A CLARION CALL BY AN IPS OFFICER

A CLARION CALL BY AN IPS OFFICER

DR. A.P. MOHAMMED ALI

KALPAZ

A Clarion Call by an IPS Officer

Rs. 750

ISBN: 81-7835-744-5

Published in 2010 in India by
Kalpaz Publications
C-30, Satyawati Nagar,
Delhi-110052
E-mail: kalpaz@hotmail.com
Phone : 9212729499

Lasser Type Setting by: Rudra Computer Graphics, Delhi
Printed at : Young Art Press, Delhi

Dedication

As a student of history I know the remarks attributed to the rule of Mughal Emperor Jahangir, "tumbled through life and tumbled out of it". Similarly 30 years of my official career had witnessed the ups and downs of my life. But my beloved wife Mrs. K.A. Methar John Begam had stood by my side as a solid as a solid rock patently as extended enormous moral support to face my upheavals while discharging the official duties. She had nurtured our four children with due care, caution and composure. Hence I dedicate this book to my loving wife.

Contents

Foreword

Brother A.P. Mohammed Ali wished me to write a foreword to his book "A Clarion Call by an IPS Officer". I could not decline for many good reasons. I am an admirer of this man in uniform for his honest service to the society at large. Though he was Deputy Commissioner at Chennai, when I was the Vice Chancellor of University of Madras, we had little or no occasion to meet and talk. But both of us had heard of good things about each other. Only when his son was enrolled in (B.S. Abdul Rahman) Crescent Engineering College, had I come close to him. I have noticed him to have an ever cheerful look and an all-time smiling face.

When I shook hand with him, I felt sponge-like softness in his palm. I wondered, how in this world, an officer serving in police uniform - soft hearted, soft spoken and soft palmed - ever could succeed! Suddenly I recalled my association with two DGPs. Mr. K. Ravindran, who inducted me as a visiting lecturer in Madras - now Anna Institute of Management was soft in heart and words but not in hands, as I know him closely, when I worked later with him as his Vice President in the Green Cross Society. But Mr. Sripal was soft equally in all respects, which I knew when he took my cause to take action on a fraud, who received money from a student for admission using my name, when I was the Director of the prestigious Madras Institute of Technology and again when he was the Chairman of Board of Studies of Jain Studies in the University of Madras. Were they not a success? Brother Mohammed Ali belongs to this clan.

I have heard, through others, of his sincerity and honesty in duty. Now I had the opportunity to witness his simplicity and humility. I was highly impressed by his generally pleasing nature.

A glance through his "Clarion" again strengthened my judgment. Earlier I had the opportunity to read his Tamil book *A Kaaki Uniform Speaks*. Though the contents are similar, this Clarion has some added values. I was not sure of the meaning of the word "Clarion". I looked in to the Oxford Advance Learner's Dictionary. It says, "loud, clear and stimulating". As a teacher, I have been using three terms to depict outreaching the audience, especially students loud—voice, bold letters and close walking. It delighted me to see a parallel in both of ours calls.

True to its title, the book is clear and stimulating. Additional materials make this English version more exciting reading than its Tamil predecessor. It reverberates his thoughts fermented and the actions shaped from his student days. That enriched his capability for leadership and finally blossomed in his official duties, with social and humanitarian consciousness, concern and responsibility.

The author has grasped well the psychology of the present day readers both young and old that they have no mind and time to read serial matters continuously and hence chose events independent of each other, narrating them briefly, interestingly and crisply.

Certain incidents are unbelievably true. They show tackling ability of difficult situations, particularly involving communal and religious elements. While tactics is said to be a short time technique to tackle only the situation on hand, it is strategy that woks to tackle issues in the long run. This experience of his in attacking problems and solving them amicably has enriched him with the thought and ability of strategic approach to such problems that may crop up in future time and again. This far sight, fore thought and advance preparation has stood in good stead for his growth. In turn it has demanded his participation to tackle serious situations that arose subsequent years. He was called by his superior officers to help some times his equal colleagues and other times even / the higher cadres, though those areas - geographical or sartorial - did not lie in his jurisdiction. People of other sister communities and religions seem to have seen in him a secular personality of just approach with open mind, honesty and sincerity. This has been the secret of his success, though he was a Muslim and Police officer in Uniform.

The Clarion Call of this Officer contains all these rich experience stuffed compactly and is a must and interesting read for everyone young and old, especially those entrusted with power and endowed with authority, to know not only how to conduct oneself, but also how not to.

I pray the Almighty to bestow on him best of His blessings.

Chennai 600 020
17 September 2008

S. Sathikh
Formerly Vice-Chancellor,
Madras University

Preface

Like a child has fascination for wearing the uniform, the craze for uniform made me to serve as a Sergeant in junior division N.C.C. at Ilayangudi Hr. Secondary School and subsequently in police department. 30 years of unstinted service in the department had seen the author in serving the different fields in maintaining the law and order, criminal investigation, narcotics intelligence, coastal security, etc. The sincerity to the job, honesty to the core and unblemished record resulted in the award of President Police Medal in 2000. But the above euphoria had lasted only up to 2004. My last period of career had seen the stained events similar to the events of the spy scandal thrown on the famous ISRO space scientist Nambi Narayanan in Kerala during 1993-1994. In the action movie 'the upright Police Officer who catches the thief will be branded as a thief' by the interested quarters. Similar things had taken in both of our lives.

The natural urge of the author with the good educational background embarked the idea of giving the best of my student days and official career in the book form. I approached Dr. S. Sathik, Formerly Vice-Chancellor of Madras University to write the forward remark while he was fasting in the month of Ramzan. But he devoted his precious time in evaluating the book and corrected even the spelling mistakes like a sincere examiner to guide his beloved student to submit the thesis for the award of the Doctorate. I have no words to express my gratefulness to him. I also extend my thanks to Prof. K. Ramana Prasad who offered the introductory remarks.

I hope that the book on hand may enthrall the readers about events leading to the ups and downs of a Senior Police Officer. Any suggestion and constructive criticism from the readers may be communicated to e-mail mdaliips@yahoo.com and they will be taken into right spirits.

A.P. Mohammed Ali

Introduction

"A Clarion Call - The Voice of an I.P.S. Officer, is an eminenty readable book authored by Mr. A.P. Mohamed Ali, I.P.S. (Retd.) A distinguished Police Officer who had received the prestigious Presiden'ts award for meritorious service in the year 2000, Mr. Mohamed Ali's narration captures the attention of the reader throughout. The lucidity of the book is no less impressive than its profounditiy.

Many incidents narrated are but a small proportion in the service of the author in the department, yet they inspire admiration and adulation. His firm commitment to work-ethos without sacrificing basic human approach is laudable and comes as a fresh air in the normally suffocative police atmosphere. His uniform courtesy to the seniors and solicitude to the subordinates should be a revlelation for any one in any official hierarchy. The book will be valuable for youngsters in any profession and also to the general public who are prone to see in the uniform donned nothing but mere exercise of authority.

Mr. Mohamed Ali's unassuming but pro-active role in many routine and exciting assignments would encourage the youngsters to firmly stand by the commitments of the noble profession without fear or favour.

Regards: K.Ramana Prasad

Formerly Professor, Dept. of. English

Madurai College.

Picture taken in 1976 as freshly recruited D.S.P

As a student of Ilayangudi School in Sivaganga District, I was an NCC cadet for three years, from 1961 to 1964, wearing khaki uniform and had the distinction of reaching the Sergeant's rank in the final year. During 1974 I had the privilege of being selected as a direct recruit Dy. S.P. This uniform was further embellished with the honour from the President for Meritorious Service in the Police services. Yet this magnificent khaki uniform was stained for a brief period of 90 days as it suffered incarceration, which I will be discussing in a separate chapter. Those days behind the bars were utilised by me to write the fragrant memories of a remarkable career cutting across a period of three decades or so. They could be seen by some as small lamps: nevertheless they dispel the darkness and shine forth in their elegance in focussing on shedding lustre and light. The small radiance emanating from these lamps of thoughts probably do not give a glitter to temple-towers... but they would not be consigned to dustbin ... For these are moral testimonies to my conscience and deeds in my official career.

I have given a brief account of events in my thirty year old bond with the Police Department. Why have I done this? I am convinced that they would serve as beacon light to the younger generation!

1

My Stint with Anti-Hindi Imposition Agitation

I had my high school education in the Ilayangudi High School, Sivaganga District till 1964 when I appeared for the final examination. I was in the school N.C.C. wing for three years and during 1963-64 attained the rank of Sergeant. Though anti-Hindi slogans were raised throughout Tamil Nadu, N.C.C. commands were only in Hindi. In the S.S.L.C. Examination we all had optional paper in Hindi: all of us had routinely written down the question paper itself as answer.

I studied the Pre-University Course in Raja Duraisingham Memorial College in Sivaganga. In January 1965, we had observed a fast against Hindi imposition. With a view to ridicule our fasting, students who were sympathetic to the Congress party had distributed hand bills criticising the agitation. At that time the news of the death of one Rajendran, son of a constable working in Sivaganga, who was studying in Annamalai University as a result of police shooting during an anti-Hindi agitation protest, provoked the whole of Tamil Nadu, particularly, Sivaganga Township. The following day students in Sivaganga took out a procession condemning the police action.

The procession was taken through the street where the police station was located and after crossing the market street reached near the palace. The police stopped the procession from going further towards the bus-stand. The students were greatly agitated and then and there burnt Hindi books and copies of government orders imposing Hindi. In order to prevent it, the police resorted to lathi-charge. The students ran helter-skelter and were scattered all over the place. Some sought refuge in the neighbouring houses. Some good householders gave protection to them. Some, however, handed over students to the police. I was one of those students who felt the brutal impact of police lathi charge that day. In fact the undesirable police oppression of that day left an indelible impression in the minds of the students. It was not a surprise that this later on sowed the seeds for sprouting of the D.M.K. rule.

A meeting to coordinate the activities of anti-Hindi imposition of the college students of the southern districts was held at Alagappa College, Karaikudi presided over by a student leader, Jeeva Kalaimani. I participated in the same as a representative of Sivaganga College. During the college holidays we arranged a conference of anti-Hindi imposition in our Ilayangudi and invited Jeeva Kalaimani and Dr. Kalimuthu (subsequently Speaker of Tamilnadu Assembly). To reach Ilayangudi one has to come from Madurai to Paramakudi. At that time due to floods in the river Vaigai, Emaneswaram Lake had breached and cut off Paramakudi-Ilayangudi road. There was a huge gap in the road where the present Gandhinagar stands. Bus traffic came to a halt. So I, lawyer Razaaq, Prof. Kadarkani and others went to the spot using bicycles, brought the dignitaries and conducted the conference.

2

Political Activities During My Student Days

During 1965 anti-Hindi agitation, as I could not concentrate on studies, I failed in the Pre-University Course examination. Thereafter I got through the examination by working hard. My father who was living in Malaysia had the dream of shaping me as a doctor. But as I had failed in the science subjects in the PUC, during 1966 I joined the Chennai New College to pursue degree course in History. I was also a hostelite at that time. I had the great fortune of imbibing learning under History Professors Buhari, Mirza, Packianathan, Abbas, English Professor Gopalakrishnan, Philosophy Professor Mohammad Kasim, Tamil Professors Kannappa Mudaliar and Cine-fame Pandurangan. Formal learning was there but the unsubsided flame of anti-Hindi imposition agitation of the students community made them give great support to D.M.K. during 1967 general elections. Perarignar DMK General-Secretary Anna contested the South Madras Parliamentary constituency against the Congress candidate, Indian Express Trade Unionist leader, Mr. Gurumurthi. As New College is situated in the Thousand Lights state legislature constituency, I had thundered in the meetings to support Anna. Anna won the M.P. seat and also and Madiazhagan, who stood as DMK candidate for assembly.

D.M.K. won a resounding victory thanks to the great student support. Many Congress leaders were defeated: even Kamaraj was defeated by a student-leader P. Srinivasan. D.M.K. ministry was constituted under Perarignar Anna. The swearing-in ceremony was held in Rajaji Hall, Mount Road where thousands of people had assembled. All the front ranking leaders of D.M.K. became ministers. The late N.V. Natarajan, a top leader of DMK, was not then included. After the swearing-in ceremony was over, we saw Anna going near N.V. Natarajan and consoling him. Later on N.V. Natarajan also got a ministerial berth when Kalaignar M. Karunanidhi formed his ministry after the demise of Anna in 1969.

The student leaders wanted somehow a representation in the Madras University. At that time the Central Government had dismissed the communist ministry of West Bengal. Along with student representatives, R. Janarthanam, Durai Murugan, Senchi Ramachandran, Jeeva Kalaimani, N.V.N. Somu, Selvam and others, I too went to Anna's residence in Nungambakkam. We were sitting in the court-yard of the house. Anna, with an unshaven face, along with other ministers, N.V.N. Govindaswamy and Kalaignar sat on a small bench facing us. After the introductions were over, on behalf of the City students, R. Janarthanam stated that a meeting on behalf of Madras University Students was to be held at S.I.E.T. auditorium and requested Anna to preside over the same. Anna accepted the same and participated in the meeting. In the welcome address R. Janarthanam put forth the idea that representation should be given for the students in the University Senate. While replying to the address Anna told the assemblage that unlike the Central Government which had dismissed the duly elected state communist party government in West Bengal, students must suggest legal means whereby solutions could be had and thus win the approval of the people for their demand. Thereafter, it was decided to hold a demonstration and meeting condemning the Central Government for dismissing the West Bengal Government. A procession was taken out from May Day Park in Chindadripet to Abbotsbury Mahal at Anna Salai near Arivalayam. A huge meeting was also held to condemn the Central Government.

Even when Anna was the Chief Minister, there took place at Venmani in Tanjore district the tragic incident of gruesome killing of more than 30 poor agriculturist labourers who had demanded higher wages. In condemning this act, Anna had stated that it was like piercing his chest with a lance. There was a debate in New College under the caption, "Is Life a Pleasure Garden or A desert?" I participated in it and quoting Venmani incident stressed that life was like a desert and got a special prize. When I was studying in the Presidency College in 1969 for post-graduation, my article on this topic was published in a students' magazine. Communist leader P. Manickam who had come to see Mr. M.T. Rajukumar at University PG Hostel called me and complimented me for the same.

3

Kalaignar's Poem on Anna's Death: Wrenched Everyone's Heart!

Arignar Anna occupied the office of Chief Minister of Tamil Nadu only for a short time. He was indisposed and passed away in 1969. Kalaignar Karunanidhi, who succeeded him, had composed an obituary poem in honour of Anna: when he read that out I know how it moved the hearts of thousands of people. There was no cooking in our New College hostel for three days as a mark of respect, after the death of Anna. In the morning we were proceeding from New College to Royapettah police station to see whether any hotel had opened for our partaking breakfast. On the way, a radio from a barber-shop was broadcasting Kalaignar's poem on Anna's passing away. We stood there, listened to the purport of the same. The barber was half-way through his job on a customer, who was shedding his tears profusely on hearing the broadcast. We could not judge whether it was due to marvellous diction of Kalaignar's poem or his great love for Anna. The poem of Kalaignar had such heart-rending impact on one and all.

I felt a similar impact when I read Kalignar's poem on Taj Mahal, published in Thina Thanthi, 11.07.07 issue. He was narrating the love of Emperor Shah Jahan on Queen Mumtaj. Some of the excerpts are... "Even when he proceeds to the battlefield, his heart never leaves his true-love for a while; When the fourteenth child was born, that lady light had shed its life's breath; remained forever the repository of unending love; she blazed forth as the great light divine of undiminished love; There...we see...Taj Mahal, the first wonder to be beholden by people of the world." If one were to state that this poem represents the Crown-Jewel on Taj Mahal, it would be no exaggeration.

4

Student Days and Inter-Religious Peace and Amity

While a student of the Presidency College for my M.A. degree, I was in what was referred to as People's lodge but officially known as Victoria Hostel during the first year, 1969 and in the Madras University Post-graduates Hostel situated in the Marina Beach during the second year, 1970. I was also elected as General Secretary of PG hostel.

On one Vinayaka Chaturthi day, a section of University Hostel inmates wanted the idol of Vinayaka to be placed on the Dining Table and breakfast with sundal be served. However another section of the students who were followers of Periyar, an atheist revolutionary, stated that if that were allowed a small statue of Periyar should also be placed on the dinner table and breakfast served. Before differences of opinion could flare up into a big quarrel, I pacified both the sections. I said dining table is meant for partaking of food alone: there was no need to place any statue or picture. What we do need is tasty dishes: we shall have sundal as well as kesari sweet. This was accepted by all.

When I served as Deputy Commissioner of Police in Chennai, during the procession of Vinayakar idols, I was asked to control the Muslim youth near Ice House Mosque. My laudable services then were greatly appreciated by former D.G.P.Vaikunth in an article in Tughlaq weekly. The experience gained there was useful to me in Kallakkurichi, Villupuram District. The unpleasant experience for both the Hindus and Muslims used to reach its great heights when Vinayaka Chaturthi is celebrated there every year. I was serving as D.I.G. of Villupuram during 2000. Hindu Munnani people wanted the Vinayaka procession to be taken through the bazaar street where there is a mosque and permit trumpet and other instruments. The Muslims would not agree to it. The district administration called both the parties for negotiations; both the sides were adamant in their arguments. Then I intervened and suggested a compromise: the mosque should be closed by 2.PM and Muslims should leave the place. The people who bring the Vinayaka idol in the procession should stop instrumental music a hundred feet before the mosque and would resume the same after 100 feet away from the mosque. This suggestion was accepted by both the parties. They invited that I should visit Kallakurichi on that day without fail. I accepted the invitation and went there. There were nearly 5,000 saffron clad members of Hindu Munnani. S.P. Mr.Ravi and Dy.S.P. Mr.Uttam Singh had made elaborate arrangements for the peaceful conduct of the event. Not only that, when the procession came to the bazaar street, we had arranged that both the parties would meet each other cordially. Accordingly leaders of Muslim community greeted Vinayaka procession organisers with garlands and special robes. They embraced each other in friendliness and the shouts of Hindu-Muslim bhai- bhai rented the air reflecting Indian culture, unity in diversity.

5

Height of Group Clashes in Congress which I Witnessed

In 1976, after finishing Police practical training in Madurai, I took charge as D.S.P. Madurai (Rural) in June. At that time Mr. P. Ramachandran was the President of Tamil Nadu Congress Committee. One of the pillars of Congress at that time was Mr.Pazha. Nedumaran. The DMK cadre was incensed that Mrs.Indira Gandhi was responsible for dismissal of their government and held a black flag demonstration in the South Veli Street when Mrs.Gandhi visited Madurai. This led to big violence and when big sticks were thrown at Mrs.Gandhi, Mr.Pazha Nedumaran bore that brunt. That is why Congressmen there called him as "Maveeran", a great hero. But as if to prove that groupism was not new to Congress, there were splits in the Madurai Congress as well. One group supported Mr.P.Ramachandran and another one Mr.Pazha Nedumaran.

In 1977 January, Mr.P. Ramachandran was due to address a number of meetings in Madurai. It was also announced that he would hoist the flag at Tirupparankundram and address the gathering. But the supporters of Mr.Pazha Nedumaran had announced that flag-hoisting and addressing the meeting would be done by him at a nearby place about the same time. We called both the parties and held talks with them at the Tirupparankudram Police Station. But both the groups were firm in their respective stand. At that time there was President's rule in Tamil Nadu and each side wanted to show off its strength.

At dusk, when Mr.P. Ramachandran was hoisting the flag, another group which had assembled at a nearby mandapam raised slogans against him. As at one stage there was stone-throwing too, the Police resorted to mild lathi-charge and prevented large scale escalation of violence.

This did not stop that. I was considered as the supporter of State Congress President group, one who belonged to Keelakkarai, also belonged to the camp of Keelakkarai smugglers etc. It was so reported to the power-centre in Chennai and I was transferred to Coimbatore City as D.S.P. Law and Order. Only after S.P. Mr.Kandasamy told them about me, then did they come to know that I belonged to Ilayangudi which is 55 km away to Keelakkarai. Still, Mr. S.P. Kandasamy asked me to be cheerful as I was after all going to Coimbatore as City DSP.

6

Governor Who Ignored Arrogant Party Men's Threat for an Official and Complimented the Official!

In 1976 the Central Government dismissed the State DMK Government during Emergency and Governor's rule was proclaimed. Mr.Mohanlal Sukhadia, who had served as Chief Minister of Rajasthan for 25 years was appointed the Governor of Tamil Nadu, He had an imposing personality.

The Governor had come to Madurai for the first time. As I was Madurai rural D.S.P., right from his entering Madurai limits to Travellers' Bungalow, I was given the responsibility of security. People had gathered enthusiastically to see the Governor on the road side. The Governor came to Travellers' Bungalow and took the police guard of honour. Then at the portico prominent citizens were introduced to him. At that time Advocate Mr. Chandran, one congress advocate from K.K. Nagar pointed out to Governor Mr. Raghupathi, I.A.S., Special Officer for Milk Producers' Union and complained that he was rejecting the petitions given by Congress party men. This made the District Collector, D.I.G., S.P. and Mr. Raghupathi frown. The

Governor, however, patted Mr.Chandran saying, “Peace, calm down!” and went inside the place allotted to him.

Thereafter Mr. Chandran and other prominent people went inside to see the Governor. The officers were in the court yard. Mr. Raghupathi, I.A.S., who had not recovered from the shock, was explaining to the other officials the reason for Mr.Chandran's anger. He said while he was having a meeting with the milk project officials one morning, without any prior announcement Mr. Chandran had come to make some recommendation. Mr.Raghupathi had sent him the message through an assistant that he would see him after the meeting. Mr. Chandran told the assistant that as he was not immediately attended to, he would do show the officer who he was. That is why he had made such remarks about him to the Governor.

When the officers were thus engaged, the people who had gone in to see the Governor returned. Mr. Chandran looked very pale, walked without much enthusiasm and got into his car. Then the officials were called in. The Governor told Mr. Raghupathi, “You go ahead with your work fearlessly; don't be bothered with recommendations.” Thus he consoled him. Then it was a revelation to us as to how he was a successful Chief Minister for 25 years. If only all administrators were like him, it is no exaggeration to say that India would have become a good and powerful country even twenty years back.

7

The Death of Cine-Fame Sando Chinnappa Thevar and Embarrassment to Police due to Indiscreet Approach

In 1978, I was serving as D.S.P. Law and Order in Coimbatore City. At that time Mr. Panchapakesan was the S.P. and he had gone for training to New Delhi. Mr.Kumarasamy who was the S.P.Rural was holding additional charge of Coimbatore City as well.

Sando Chinnappa Thevar was a famous actor director in Tamil cine field. His house was in Ramanathapuram of Coimbatore City. Shooting work was going on for one of his films in Ooty. Sando who had been there had a massive heart attack and suddenly passed away. The body was brought to his house and it was announced that the funeral procession would take place the following morning by 10.

As Chinnappa Thevar was very popular, we expected a very large number of cine actors and accordingly made security arrangements. Around 7.00 p.m. the news came that the cine fame Chief Minister of Tamil Nadu, M.G.R. would be arriving for the funeral procession. We swung into action combined the urban and rural police force and made elaborate security arrangements one for procession from Sando's house till the burial ground and the other general security arrangements. As many V.I.P.s and cine stars were coming, Mr.Kumarasamy S.P., I and Inspector Duraisamy went to Chinnappa Thevar's house and discussed matters pertaining to security with his younger brother and cine director Mr.Tirumugam.

The S.P. told Mr.Tirumugam that as the Chief Minister and popular cine stars were coming by plane in the morning security arrangements were necessary and asked Mr.Tirumurgam to arrange for proper wooden fencing around the house and also in the road leading to the funeral ground. Mr. Tirumugam who was very patient till then lost his temper and said, "Sir, we are in deep grief due to the death of Sando Thevar. We are not sure about his income or expenditure and are worried accordingly. You want us to spend some money for security. We are not interested in MGR or any other actor. We will manage the funeral." We came out with S.P. who was very much shocked at what he heard and told him, "Sir, if we talk about expenses in a bereaved house, they would not accept the same: only we have to bear it." He said that there was no provision for government spending on private individual's activities." Then we acquainted the matter with the District Collector and the P.W.D. officials. It was decided to construct suitable protective barricades as part of security arrangements for the Chief Minister. Everything was completed in the night itself. In the morning when Mr. M.G.R. and a number of cine actors also participated in the procession and finally in the rites, all arrangements had been suitably made. Nothing untoward happened.

From the above, we learnt that one has to be discreet as to our suggestions taking into account the time and place.

8

Participation in Cultural Functions Along with Cine Stars and Unnecessary Sensation

During 1977-1980, when I was working as D.S.P. Coimbatore City I used to participate in many cultural functions. Once in 1979 there was an evening cultural function of "Urvasi". The District Collector Mr.Sivaprakasam, Auditor Mr. C. G. Venkataramanan and I attended the same. Cine stars Rajinikant, Latha, Sripriya and many famous cine actors and actresses were also present. As I was in the same stage, I was conversing with them. They said that that had come for a shooting of a film and were put up at Alankar Hotel in Ram Nagar.

Next morning two Inspectors from CID came to my office. Assuming that they would have come for giving some important news I asked as usual, "Anything special?" They said, "Sir, You were speaking with cine people yesterday in Urvasi recreation cultural function. Did they mention anything special as to where they were going today?" I said, "They did not say anything important. Nor did I ask as to where they were going today. We just talked about cultural events." Then I asked as to why they were asking that question. They said that in Alankar College an important actor and a prominent actress are missing. So people have asked from Chennai to find out their whereabouts. We asked whether we should search for them. But they replied that there was no need and that they would sort it out. Then they left the place requesting me not to divulge this information to anyone. After two days I chanced to meet those Inspectors. I asked about what happened to the missing artists. They said that the sensational cine couple went to Palani and were to have got married, but on orders from Chennai they could stop that and sent loade the acters to chennai.

From this I learnt that officials should be very cautious while moving with these personalities.

9

Police-Public Community Service

I was serving as Dy. Superintendent of Police (Law and Order), Coimbatore City from 1977 to 1980. I had then devised a plan to integrate the services of the students with the services of the police force. Each college would have a National Social Service camp where the students would be asked to perform nearly 15 days' services in the villages. At the end of the camp, they will be given a Certificate. When they seek a job, this certificate becomes a valuable testimony.

I thought that the same N.S.S. students could have a camp in the Coimbatore City and working along with the police could do service to the people. Accordingly I approached the N.S.S. co-ordinates of the city colleges during 1979. They also agreed to abide by my suggestion. The leaders of N.S.S. students' wing like Manohar and Jayakumar integrated the services of the students. They joined hands with the police during the latter's night patrolling and also during day time assisted in the activities of the policy by helping them to round up pocket-pickers, assisting in the traffic control, etc. They occupied themselves like this for 15 days. Their capabilities in these fields matched those of police personnel. The public and the press very much appreciated the project.

At the end of the 15 days' camp, a function was organised in R.S. Puram Municipality Auditorium to award certificates to N.S.S. students. The great patron of education in Coimbatore at that time (late) Thru G.R. Damodaran, who was then the Vice-Chancellor of Madras University presided over the function, appreciated the work of the students and awarded the certificates.

I had then moved to many places. In 1991 while I was working as Chennai North Law and Order Deputy Commissioner, the then Chief Minister Selvi Jayalalitha hoisted the National flag at the fort and distributed food packets to the disabled. It was there that I saw Mr. Jayakumar who was the Co-ordinator of the N.S.S. activities in Coimbatore, after a gap of 11 years. I asked him as to where he was serving. He said that he was working as a Project Officer in Social Welfare Board. He also informed that when he appeared for interview for this post, the certificate we had issued in 1979 for his Coimbatore work was of great help and expressed his gratitude for the same. It gave me a sense of fulfilment.

10

1979 Police Strike and help Rendered by Karate Exponents

The year 1979 was a turbulent one for the Police force. Even though we have got freedom, the Police Act of 1861 left by the British is still the basis administration for police force. When the Britishers were there, Indian policemen were largely used to serve their personal domestic needs. Even after independence, politicians and higher police officials had treated the constables as unannounced slaves only and suppressed their rights. For example, the constables had to sweep the houses of higher officials, iron the clothes of officials and their dependents, polish the shoes of officials, and do the cleaning of vessels in the household, look after the gardens of the officials' residences as unpaid labour and the like. The officials had no qualms in ordering the constables to do all these works. If any constable dared to question the nature of work or utter disagreeable words or showed dissenting signs, he was given punishment in the form of more physical exercises, night patrolling, and even punishments based on false charges. The constables, therefore, were patiently doing all these odd jobs. They did not have any proper organisation to protect their rights or redress their grievances. However, standing orders in the department are specific that higher officials on inspection must hear the grievances of the constables and rectify the same: but this was only a paper relief. Rarely do we find any instance of officials resorting to this step to address the grievances of the constables. The higher officials did not appreciate the fact that the very long standing grievances of the constables had reached a smouldering point and could flare up at any time.

During 1975, Mrs. Indira Gandhi the Prime Minister proclaimed an Emergency Rule for the whole of the country. Efforts were on to break the shackles on freedom by the people who rose in great rebellion under the leadership of Jayaprakash Narayan. In 1977 Emergency was withdrawn and in the elections that soon followed Janata Party under the leadership of Morarji Desai formed the government at the Centre. In Tamil Nadu, too, during 1977 elections Bharat Ratna M.G.R. formed the ministry. At that time Mr. E.L. Stracey, an Anglo-Indian, was the Director General of Police and Mr. Senthamarai was the Inspector General of Police.

In 1979 the Central Reserve Police constables organised a struggle throughout the country to protect their rights. The fiery struggle found its echo in Tamil Nadu as well where also the agitation had spread. At that time I was functioning as Deputy Superintendent, Law and Order, of Coimbatore City. A number of secret meetings of Tamil Nadu Special Police Force camp were held under Havildars Perumal and Sundaram at Kovai Pudur near Coimbatore. In Coimbatore City proper they went on strike under the leadership of Head Constable Sattaiwar Palanichamy. Mr. Neiwal was SP, Mr. Pandian was Dy. S.P of Pappanaickanpalayam. Mr. Sitaraman was the D.I.G. then. Constables who were proceeding to the houses of police officials in places like Madukkarai and Pappanaickanpalayam were intimidated along with constables in the police stations to join the strike. The strike was taken advantage of by Coimbatore

Peelaimedu area Ramakrishna Mills where two factions of brothers-owners were about to come to blows posing grave threat to general peace and order. Even though C.R.P.F. and B.S.F. were present, their strength was not much. Some CRPF constables sympathised with the constables' strike and refused to perform their duties. But B.S.F. personnel co-operated fully with the officials. At that time Mr. Vasanth, the brother of Karate Mani, who had popularised this self-protection martial art in Tamil Nadu, was giving training to youngsters in the Y.M.C.A. Coimbatore. I was also taking lessons for some months. I asked Vasanth whether he would come along with his trainees to work together with police officials.

He agreed and a hand-picked 50 karate trained people helped the police force in Coimbatore City and also prevented the major group clashes in Ramakrishna Mills. Thus we could effectively function during that crisis.

On that occasion 700 constables belonging to Kovai Pudur Special police force under the leadership of Perumal assembled at Gandhipuram Bus stand to take out a procession even as the whole city came to a stand still. Under the headship of Mr. Neilwal, S.P, we stopped that procession near Kovai Women's Polytechnic. The Special Police force insisted that they too should be arrested and they would not disperse. At that time in the camp office of D.I.G. Mr. Sitaraman, Special Police force Commander Mr.Veeraraghavan was also there. D.I.G. Mr. Sitaraman got in touch with Mr.Neilwal through wireless and said that higher officials in Madras did not want to arrest Special Police force but just disperse them by using force through lathi-charging. Mr. Neilwal asked my opinion with the words, "What do you say?" I said that the striking policemen too had democratic rights and they wanted to be arrested. Then why should we lathi-charge them? Mr. Nielwal agreed with me and told D.I.G. Mr. Sitaraman, "Sir, we are on the spot. Our decision will only be correct." Then he asked me to arrest them. I told the striking policemen that we did not have enough vehicles and that there were placed under arrest and that all of them would peacefully march towards the Central Jail which was nearby. This appeal was made by me through the loud-speakers. They obeyed in a much disciplined manner and proceeded towards the Central Jail.

All the arrested constables had been stationed in a nearby auditorium. But when they were asked to give out their names, and physical identification marks before being lodged in the prison, they refused to do so. They clamoured that the prison gates be opened and all of them simultaneously let in. I and Mr. Hutchinson, who was then Jail Superintendent at that time read out to them the relevant portion of the jail manual as to how that could not be done. Those arrested before they are sent to the prison must sign or their fingerprint taken and force could be used to obtain the same if they refused to cooperate. According to prison rules a prisoner comes under the authority of the jail officials once he has been remanded to custody. The constables of Special Reserve Force understood the significance of this and agreed to give out their names and identification. Then one by one they gave their names and the process of putting them in prison continued throughout the night.

M.G.R. who understood the reasonableness in the demands of the constables not only ordered all of them to be released but reinstated them in the jobs. He felt that the approach of the department in this regard was not proper and that was why the constables had to resort to the strike. He made efforts to redress their grievances and shifted DGP and IGP by posting Mr. T.T.P. Abdullah as DGP and Mr. Pon Paramaguru as IGP.

11

Police-Public Goodwill Sports Competition

I was working as Dy.S.P. (Law and Order) in Coimbatore from 1977 to 1980. At that time a number of violent agriculturists' agitations under Mr. Narayanasamy Naidu, Mr. Chinnasamy Gounder and Mr. Nataraja Gounder were taking place. Coimbatore, which is often described as South Indian Manchester which has a number of cotton mills. Every year two months before Deepavali bonus disputes would start. Under the leadership various labour unions namely INTUC Mr. P.L Subbiah, HMS Mr. A. Subramaniam, on behalf of Janata Dal Sengaliappan, who was also known as 'Kovai Kamaraj' and Mr.Ramraj, DMK Mr. Doraisamy, AIADMK Messrs.U.R. Krishnan, Singanallur Karuppasamy, CITU Mr.Bhoopati, AITC Mr. Nanjappan workers would be participating in demonstrations and strikes. Similarly there would be demonstrations and strikes pertaining to Provident Fund, E.S.I. etc. The students also would go on strike demanding free bus basses; under the leadership of Mr. Bose of SFI. There were strikes in schools and colleges and stone throwing incidents as well. I had the responsibility to see that the situation did not go out of control though I had only a limited number of constables. The general public also had displeasure with police as the latter had gone on strike during 1979.

One day Mr. J.P. Joseph who was Vice-Principal when I was undergoing DSP training in Vellore Police Training School, and who also had participated in 1957-58 Olympic games as an athlete came to see me. I was discussing the nature of problems in Coimbatore City. He then said, "You are a sportsman. Why don't you conduct sports for police-public to generate general goodwill?" He had seen me playing foot-ball and kabbadi with constables in the training school. I thought that was a good idea and decided to implement the same. I formed a "Police-Public Sports Committee". Dr. Baktavatsalam, Director of K.G. Hospital, Senior Advocate Mr. Mayilsamy, Industrialists Mr. Nanjundan, Everest Engineering proprietor Mr. Somasundaram and Area Commander of Home Guards Mr. Varadarajan took leading part in this venture.

It was decided to have Sports for one selected section of people once in two months and one industrialist would distribute the prizes to the victors. The first sports meet of Students and Police was held at P.S.G. Arts College. The principal of that college Mr.T.K.P.Varadarajan presided over the meet. Next meet was between the Police and the labourers on May Day which was held at Coimbatore Armed Reserve grounds. The next one was arranged between the Police and agriculturists in Karamadai, a village on the way to Ooty. The president of Agriculturists Association Mr. Narayanasamy Nayudu's son Mr. Nandagopal, leaders Mr. Nataraja Gounder and Mr. Chinnasamy Gounder, all graced the occasion.

When the news of successful Police-Public sports meet at Coimbatore, with the enthusiastic response of general public, labourers, agriculturists and students leading to very smooth relationship between the public and police reached the ears of the then DGP Mr. E.L. Stracey, he honoured me by making me a Member of Police Sports Control Board; though there were many ranking higher officials in that board, I, a Dy. S.P. was also given a proud place in it. When an All-India Police Sports meet took place at Chennai in 2002 and brought out a souvenir on the occasion, Mr. J. P. Joseph mentioned in it as follows: "The present D.I.G. Mr. Mohamed Ali, while functioning as a Dy. S.P. in Coimbatore had distinguished himself. The former Director General of Police, Mr. E. L. Stracey recognising his invaluable service made him a member of State Police Sports Control Board. In one of the Police-Public sports meets in Coimbatore, a handicapped boy (having lost an arm) came first in the high-jump competition: many mentally disabled children participated and enjoyed the kabbadi games during that time. These are unforgettable events."

12

Deranged Attitude of an S.P. (When one has to Face Annihilation, his Mind becomes Deranged –Vinasa Kale Vipareeda Buddihi)

I was working as Dy. S.P. in Coimbatore City from 1977 to 1980. The office of the S.P. was in the first floor and mine was on the ground floor. The Press is often referred to as the Fourth Eye of a Democratic state: some of the important correspondents of prominent papers were Mr.Padmanabhan and Mr.Venugopal from The Hindu, Mr. Janakiraman of PTI, Mr. Gopal of The Indian Express, Mr. Peter of Thina Thanthi, Mr. Jawahar of Dinakaran, Mr. Babu, Mr. Ramamurthy of Makkal Kural, Mr. Ramasamy of Dina Malar, Mr. Amin of Malai Murasu. All gathered and provided 'hot news' to people in a very attractive way. They were all very friendly and understanding. They cooperated amongst themselves and gathered news feverishly. They also acted as a good bridge between the police and the public. As the City Dy. S.P.'s office was in the ground floor, they would come there and collect important news.

A new S.P. had assumed office. All correspondents paid a courtesy call to him. One correspondent shook S.P.'s hands and instead of customary lemon, gave him a mango. The S.P. was not very happy about it. They asked him about future plans. This generally happens whenever a new S.P. takes charge and when the correspondents pay a courtesy call. The new S.P. was irritated at some of the questions of the correspondents. But he did not show it outwardly.

One day on his way to his office, the S.P. had seen a group of journalists entering my room on the ground floor. After some time I received a note from him stating that correspondents need not be unnecessarily permitted in the office. I personally went to his office and told him that the journalists have been good to us and inform the public about our varied and constructive activities and unlike in some districts where false and vicious news about police are put out, these correspondents have been very helpful. I also submitted a written reply to his note.

After many weeks, the S.P. held a press meet. At that time, Mr. Venugopal of The Hindu wanted some clarifications. He also suggested that it would be good if the District S.P. were to hold a press meet once a week. But the S.P. said it was enough if they came whenever summoned. That reply was not liked by them.

Next day there was a meeting of Dy.S.P.s. The S.P. asked me, "Ali, why this Hindu correspondent has been asking inconvenient questions?" I said that it was possible that sometimes we may not like their questions but without getting angry, it would be better if we manage them. But he said, "One should place some ganja (narcotics) in the scooter where such people travel, put them 'in' for a couple of days. Then they will be docile." All of us were shocked to hear this. I told him smilingly, "There are instances where even governments have fallen due to the press. So, please don't entertain such dreams." As the dialogue took place in the Dy.S.P.s. meeting, the correspondents came to know about it. It was with great difficulty that I could pacify them. After a brief period, that S.P. had left Coimbatore.

13

D.G.P.E.L. Stracey's Guidance to the Younger Generation of Police Establishment

When I was the Dy. S.P. of Coimbatore City in 1978, Mr. Abdullah was the Dy. S.P. of the Crime Branch. Both of us were youngsters. Mr. T. Manoharan was S.P. Coimbatore South.

Once Mr.E.L. Stracey, an Anglo-Indian, who was the Director General of Police paid a short visit to Coimbatore and had left for Wellingdon, Nilgiris Dist. immediately. He was a man of simple habits. In Vellore Police Training school, in 1975 when we were in the Officers' Mess, Mr.Stracey had come there, touched a pillar, found it covered with dust and expressed his unhappiness over it. He always expected every activity of ours should be fully within law. He wanted that the police officers should be role models to youngsters.

Whenever he visited a place he did not want higher officials to meet him at the railway station. He also insisted that no officials should wait for him at the place where he was staying. On returning from Wellington, Ooty, before proceeding to Madras, he was to take rest in English Club near Coimbatore

Govt. Arts College. I and Mr. Abdullah told Mr.Manoharan, "Sir, we want to pay a courtesy call on Mr. Stracey." He hesitated a little but acceded to our request. The three of us went to the English Club and had been waiting there. When we got the information through wireless that the DGP's car had entered into Coimbatore City, the SP told us, "If you are found here, DGP will take me to task. You better go the backside of the English Club." Then he added, "You come to his room, after he finishes his cup of tea." We accordingly went to the backyard of the club. Exactly at 7.00 P.M. Mr.Stracey's car entered the club premises. Mr.Stracey had noticed us in the headlights thrown by the car. When the car reached the portico, the S.P. received him. But instead of going to his room, Mr.Stracy came to the place where we were hiding and smiled, "Come on my dear boys! Why are you hiding? I am not a lion or a tiger!" So saying he put his hands on our shoulders and led us to his room.

He offered us tea and only when we finished it, he himself drank tea. Then he told the S.P. that he should give the youngsters good guidance. He asked about the details of work we were doing. Then he left for Madras. He thus showed how senior officials should guide the younger officials along proper lines.

14

Policemen Families' Welfare Activities

When I was Dy.S.P. in Coimbatore City during 1977 to 1980, we made arrangements for the families of policemen to have get-together once a month. These meetings were held at the place where the present Corporation Commissioner's office is situated. We arranged running races for children, competition in fancy dress, musical chairs, separate games and sports for girls, besides music and dance and drama competitions.

Thereafter when I was functioning as Superintendent of Police in Salem in 1986, I learnt that there was severe water shortage, almost a famine, in the Reserved Force grounds. I learnt that there were just two wells in the ground and womenfolk were drawing water only from these two wells. I met the District Collector Captain Thangadurai and through him was able to arrange installation of two motor pumps for drawing out water, which mitigated the sufferings of the families of policemen.

Once I was invited by the Secretary of Tiruchengode Gandhi Ashram, Mr.Aravamudan to see the activities going on there. When I was there, he explained how womenfolk are taught book-binding, making of incenses, matches, candles, extracting oil from ground-nut cakes, spinning of khaddar cloth and similar skills in cottage industries sector. I asked him whether it would be possible for him to impart such instruction to womenfolk in police quarters so that they could gain part-time employment. He readily agreed to it. Accordingly I arranged some of the part-time jobs of Gandhi Ashram like book-binding, candle-making etc. to be done by womenfolk of police quarters which enabled them to earn some additional income for the family.

From January to May 1987 I was serving as the Commandant of Tamil Nadu Special Police Force at Veerapuram near Avadi, Chennai. The Vice-Principal of my former Police Training Institute Mr. J.P. Joseph was also serving there. Avadi and Veerapuram areas were very dry and families of police force faced great difficulties on that account. I and Mr. Joseph met with Mr.Pandian, I.A.S., who was the Collector of Chengalpat District we met him in Panagal Buildings, Saidapet and represented the matter. Mr.Pandian immediately ordered R.D.O. and Tahsildar of Avadi area to dig 3 open wells in Avadi and two for Veerapuram which alleviated the drinking problems of Police families.

15

Country Revolver Certified as Genuine Webly Scott.

I was DSP Law and Order, Coimbatore City, which is called as the Manchester of South, because of the existence of number of textile mills, ginning factories and foundries.

Dewan Bahadur Road in R.S. Puram is a posh locality. There were number of shopping complex on both sides of the road. There was an ice cream parlour owned by Chinnaswamy (name changed). His brother-in-law, Muthusamy (name changed) who was a drunkard, had a family problem and was not well disposed of with Chinnaswamy. One evening at about 7 pm the Police control room at Coimbatore received a distress phone call telling that there was a shooting incident at Ice cream parlour. Inspector Mr. Kamban and I rushed to the spot with a police party. We saw onlookers staring at Ice cream parlour which was adorned with white glass in the front. I could see an uneasy calm prevailing inside the parlor. We took position with arm and started moving slowly toward the parlour. When we opened the door we found Chinnasamy found lying slumped on the table with the pool of blood and Muthusamy on the floor blood trickling in the mouth. A revolver was also found near the right hand of Muthusamy.

We traced the parlour bearer quickly and he narrated the sad incident. Muthusamy, entered the parlour when there were few customers sitting on the chairs. He shouted at Chinnasamy telling that he was mainly responsible for spoiling his family and before anyone could realise, Muthusamy took the revolver from his pant pocket and started at firing point blank on the face of Chinnasamy resulting his scream and fell on the cash table. The customers ran away from the parlour and took shelter on the opposite side of the road.

Muthusamy took out a pocket of cyanide from shirt pocket and swallowed resulting in his instantaneous death. We checked the gun licences of the Coimbatore but there was no licence granted to Muthusamy. The scene revolver was sent to Chennai for forensic opinion. The report stated that the offence weapon was a genuine Colt make. Then we started making extensive enquiries about the source of the weapon.

For the past six months we could not get any clue. We stumbled upon an informant telling that a middle aged man was searching a prospective buyer of a revolver. We made a police constable, named, Chandran to pose as a buyer. The sale price was fixed at Rs.10000/ and the place of transaction was also fixed at the railway track behind Chintamani co-operative supermarket. At the dust of the fateful day we had taken position to trap the culprit. The disguised police constable, Chandran, was waiting with a black rexine travelers' back stuffed with white papers covered with real currencies.

The suspected middle aged man approached Chanran with nervous and received the rexine bag and opened the zip but did not count. After seeing the real currencies on the top of the bag, handed over a paper pocket to Chandran, who opened the pocket and found a revolver and then signalled to us. We surrounded the middle aged man, Thangaraj, of Kamarajpuram in Coimbatore. He was a black smith having a small work shop in front of his tiled house. After apprehending him, we quickly moved into his house and started checking. We were amazed to see that there were number spare parts of revolver. We also found an English magazine in which the manufacture and assembling techniques of a revolver was described. Then we found the pellet holes in the rear inside mud wall of the house.

The interrogation of Thangaraj reveals that he learnt the blacksmith work from his late father. One day he came across the English magazine which described the method of the various components of a revolver. He hit upon an idea of making on with his ingenious method. He had also manufactured such one. Then he wanted to test the revolver. Since his house was located in a colony where there number of houses located nearby, no one heard the sound of the revolver shot. So he used to start his Enfield motor cycle parked in front of his house by making loud noise. Then he used test the revolver by firing on the rear inside wall of his house by using the pellets. He gave the first revolver to Muthusamy the assailant of Chinnaswamy.

Then we sent the gun seized from Thangraj to Forensic test at Chennai Lab. The result showed that it was a country gun. Then we sent both, gun seized form the ice cream parlor and gun seized from Thangaraj for the lab test. The result came astonishingly stating that both guns were one and the same 'Country make colt guns'.

It shows sometimes the results of forensic labs may give the misleading results. But the Astute Investigation Officer should analyse the evidence scientifically and strenuously. Then only the realities of the complicated cases will be detected.

16

Love Leads to Misery

Love has many regretful ends and few happy moments. The psychologists will proclaim that love is a fascination and temporary physical attachment. They may also say that love is blind, has no eyes. But the teenagers may expound a dissenting note to the contest the arguments of the psychologist.

I have two incidents of solid nature in which love led to detestable end.

(1) I was DSP Madurai Rural in 1976. Arun (name changed), a first year Rajaji Medical College student had intense love affair with a school drop out, Regina (name changed). Both of them had intense attachment. On the fateful day Arun did not attend the Medical College. He took Regina to Viraganur Dam, in Silaiman Police Station limit. Viraganur Dam is situated 10KM from Madurai. On both sides of the river there are lots of coconut groves. Arun and Regina entered into one of the coconut groves in the morning and they were chit-chatting till evening. Their closeness exceeded to the physical contact. The leaves of coconut tree served as bed.

Some of the local youth, who had gone to the river via coconut grove, to take bath after day's hard work, found them in a compromising condition. The lust for sex stimulated them with bad thinking. They conspired together. They came near to them. They tied Arun in a coconut tree and indulged in forceful raping of Regina. After reducing her to the position of a torn cloth, untied the hands of Arun and threatened both not to reveal the incident to anyone. Both of them left the place with rude shock and returned to their home speechless and dazed.

A whisper campaign was going rounds in Viraganur village about the incident. It came to the ears of SI Mr. Prabakaran of Silaiman P.S. who informed Inspector Mr. Periasamy and then to me. We descended on the village, caught hold of all the five assailants. After usual police treatment they admitted their crime. The boy and the girl were traced then but both of them refused to prefer a complaint fearing that their future will be spoiled. But Arun, who took Regina to Viraganur Dam, refused to give life to her in spite of the best efforts. Even though the assailants were sent for remand, the life of the poor dropout was doomed.

(2) Another incident took place at Coimbatore in 1977. There was a famous heart surgeon, Devadoss (name changed). He had only one daughter, Meena (name changed). She was studying in the second year Home Science degree course in a college at R.S.Puram. Daily she used to take town bus from Race course, near her residence, to her college which was 3KM.away .Rajesh (name changed) was hailing from a poor farmer's family at Pollachi rural area. He had studied up to school level and joined as a conductor in a state transport company. He was staying along with two other colleagues in a small room at Mettupalayam road, RS. Puram. Meena used to go to the college in which Rajesh was the conductor. Rajesh made friendship with Meena by exchanging love letters. But she never absented herself from the college. Some of her close friends knew about the love affair but not her parents.

One evening Meena did not turn to her residence after the college hours. Her doctor father made frantic search in the college and also in the residences of her classmates without any clue. The doctor turned to me saying some rowdy gang roaming around the college would have kidnapped his daughter. We immediately swung into action. Inspector Mr. Kamban was summoned and he was given the assignment of making effective enquiries with Meena's close friends. The enquiries with one of them led to a lead that one conductor was friendly with Meena. By this time darkness had set in. But we were able to locate quickly the name of the conductor and the place of his stay.

When the police party swooped on the room of Rajesh, his room mate, another conductor was present. He told that Rajesh brought a girl by 6 p.m and wanted to stay there for the night. But he was advised against it and the room warned him to send back the girl. But Rajesh left the room along the girl by taking only a brief case telling that he was going to his native place. Inspector Mr. Kamban rushed to Rajesh's native village. He found both of them in a small hut. In fact Rajesh's father advised his son and Menna against their decision of coming there. But Meena insisted that she would stay there only or would commit suicide. The father had narrated that to Mr. Kamban. Anyhow both of them were brought to Coimbatore the following morning. Dr. Devadoss and his wife were summoned. On seeing Meena with a conductor boy, Dr. Devadoss fainted in my office. He was given first aid and became conscious. He had fainted because he could not believe that his most loved daughter would elope with a conductor. Dr. Devadoss and his wife appealed Meena to go with them forgetting her eloping as a bad dream and continue her college study. But she stoutly refused their request.

Further she argued that she was a major and she knew how to manage her future. Rajesh's father told Meena that her marriage with that boy would not suit the family status. Further it would be difficult to make both ends meet if they started living in his village. But Rajesh and Meena told that their love was eternal and needed nobody's support. Dr. Devadoss and his wife left the office when they heard them telling that they would

perform last rites. Rajesh and Meena had also left. An enquiry about the eloping and misconduct by Rajesh was conducted by the management of the transport company and Rajesh was sacked from the post. Rajesh settled Meena in his native village. Rajesh could not get proper employment. It drove him towards addiction to drinking, which was not expected by Menna. When the conduct of Rajesh became unbearable for Meena, she committed suicide.

The above two incidents are just like the tips of the iceberg of the love of misguided youth. The parents should be extra careful with their wards so that they do not venture out and fall prey to the evil designs of love.

17

Crimes, a Mirror of the Society's Image

In 1940, the population of India was 36 crores. But today it has reached nearly 110 crores. At that time cities had a population between 2 and 8 lakhs of people. However, today we find the figure has gone up from 25 to 80 lakhs. There facilities are very poor for people migrating from villages to cities. Therefore, we find many small colonies springing up everywhere, cramped cottages or dwellings, unsanitary conditions and crowded localities. There are no recreational activities, or sports and games, or even good road facilities for people living in these areas. People living in such dense areas are exposed to bad habits like resort to liquor, narcotics and gambling and indulge in such evil practices.

Circumstances lead people to indulge in crime; also they are stimulated by a desire to accumulate wealth through easy means in quick time. The fact that one can escape the consequences of crime also leads to increase in crimes. Formerly there were fewer police stations and police personnel. But now there has been increase in both. But there is a decline in the rate of prevention of crimes, watch over the criminals and detection of crimes. The reason for this is improper maintenance of records in police stations about the criminals, nature of the crimes, places where crimes are committed, etc. For example when a criminal moves out from one police jurisdiction to the other, details about him are not informed to other stations. Similarly the crimes he commits outside are not informed to police station of his original place. The records such as bad character (BCR. A.B) are not maintained properly. As a result many criminals escape from observation. Sometimes they are murdered as well.

Similarly, when the criminals are brought to the courts or when the hearings take place, the local stations do not watch much about criminals, their friends, relations, witnesses, etc. This leads to some crimes. An example is the murder of one Vijayakumar, an accused right before the Judge in the Court when the case was being heard at Egmore. One Thangapandian, an accused in murder case was being taken to Tuticorin Court but was murdered on the way. When Ayothikuppam Veeramani was being brought to Madras High Court, an attempt was made to kill him: but he managed to rush towards the dais where the Hon'ble Judge was seated and therefore managed to avoid being killed! That was the reason for opening a Police Station in the High Court campus in 1993. In 1991, a U.N.O. resolution on crimes perpetrated by a group stated that people who conspire to murder, loot, thieving, abduction, rape, kidnapping and similar acts of violence should deemed to have committed a joint crime and such collective action must be termed as gang act.

During the British rule efforts were made to deal with such gang acts. A 'Thugs Act' was passed to deal sternly with the gang of thugs who were playing havoc with the lives of the people indulging in robbery and murder. Similarly a particular group of people were declared prone to criminal acts and they were referred to as 'notified tribe'.

In Mumbai city there were people, who formed gangs and committed crimes: Some of them were Vardaraja Mudaliar, Haji

Inauguration of Madras High Court Police Station by Chief Justice Ratnam

Masthan, Yusuf Patel, Dawood Ibrahim and Chotta Rajan. In New Delhi there were Tyagi, Dinesh Srivatsava alias Patlu. In Chennai North there were Boxer Vadivelu, Malaikkan Selvam, Radhakrishnan, Elumalai, Sargunam, Kutti, Welding Kumar, Chera, Vellai Ravi, Asai, Kattan Subramaniam: In South Chennai the list included Veeramani, Kamaraj, Kapilan, Bunk Kumar, etc.

Generally these gangs indulge in the following crimes: (1) Brewing illicit liquor, (2) Dealing in Narcotics, (3) Stealing oil, (4) Pilfering rice from ration shops, (5) adulteration of cement, tobacco, pulses and oil, (6) smuggling carried out in ports, airports etc. (7) dealing in black money, (8) smuggling gold, silver, (9) smuggling sandalwood and red wood, (10) encroachment of public lands, (11) organising prostitution.

People who form gangs and commit crimes, even when put in prison manage to live in all comforts. Their families are sufficiently taken care of by their associates. Even from inside the prison, these people direct criminal operations outside because they are assisted by a number of people in the prisons. To prevent such occurrences, CCTV Cameras must be installed to monitor all cells and close scrutiny of visitors must be made. Convicts and persons under judicious custody must be given sufficient works involving physical labour. Experts in psychology must counsel these people after going through their record of crimes and suggest suitable guidelines. Voluntary social welfare organisations must come forward to rehabilitate in appropriate ways the reformed criminals: Banks also could help them to start small-scale trade etc.

Not only in Chennai but throughout Tamil Nadu crimes are committed by gangs under the control Thangaian, Mambattian, Veerappan, Seevalaperi Pandi and Paruthiyooran. Also John Pandian, Suba.Ilavarasan, Coovagam Ramasamy, Egg Ravi, Manalmedu Sankar were also some leading gangsters.

In Uttar Pradesh an act was passed in 1986 to suppress such people who organise gangs and operate. In Maharashra a similar act was passed in 1999 called Organised Crime (Prevention) act. In Andhra Pradesh a similar act came into effect. In Tamil Nadu during 2002 a bill was introduced in the Assembly; but it has not been passed till now. If that act were to be passed there is the possibility of reduction in serial-killing incidents, robberies, smuggling, abduction of persons, encroachment of public lands etc. But one must ensure that such act should not be misused by political bigwigs.

(1) Monitoring the criminals: There are two types of record books maintained to monitor criminals in police stations There are separate lists (Sheets) of rowdies and KDs for monitoring. Generally rowdies would be checked during day time and KDs. during night time. As a result those who indulge in violence, suspected murderers and smugglers are not monitored during night time. The police standing orders must be so amended to include these categories to monitor during night time as well.

(2) Constables should have visual and pro-active policing. During day time law and order division constables should join the traffic constables and have monitoring activities.

(3) In areas where people assemble for entertainment, police presence is a must.

(4) In all important traffic junctions and business complexes, CCTV must be installed.

(5) Helicopters can also be used for highways patrolling which would prevent criminals escaping.

(6) To protect ships reaching the ports from the avaricious high-sea robbers, modern patrol boats should be pressed into service.

(7) Community Service centres must be encouraged and the cooperation of general public enlisted.

(8) Efforts must be made to identify genuine informers; their services must be utilised and they must be handsomely rewarded.

(9) Global positioning system, Geographical survey system and the likes must be installed in police stations so that

jurisdictions are properly defined; details about the crimes and criminals are gathered and saved in a data base.

(10) Above all, Police Officers must have as their guiding principles justice, straight forwardness, physical agility and mental alertness. This would lead to great reduction in crimes.

18

The Suppression of Chennai Dada

If South and Central Chennai are occupied by the affluent citizens, North Chennai is primarily the abode of the working class. People belonging to lower economic strata like fishermen, labourers abound here. There are slums, dense population in the area and widespread unemployment prevails in the place. As a result it became a haven for rowdies and dadas. If you categorise the leaders of rowdies, there were many groups. One group under the leadership of Elumalai of Vanniar caste exercised its authority in the Vannarappettai-Royapuram area; Radhakrishnan of Nadar community and his brothers controlled a segment; Chinna Logu and Peria Logu belonging to Adi Dravida community held their sway in one area; in Kasimedu fishermen's are one Boxer Vadivelu with his group ruled over; then there was Malaikkan Selvam: in Vyasarpadi Subbiah along with Chera constituted a group; in the same area Vellai Ravi controlled a group. All these groups indulged in illicit brewing of liquor, fermented rice gruel (Sundi Soru) and smuggling of drugs and narcotics. As there were clash of interests in collection of mamools of these rowdies from many sources, there were frequent incidents of violence, daylight robberies, abduction of people and the like.

Mr. Radhakrishna Raja was my one of my predecessor in Vannarapettai as A.C. Between 1975 and 1979. Guru and Sargunam were the prominent rowdies who were conducting illegal betting on races, operations of pocket-picking, brewing of illicit liquor etc. They were also collecting mamools from lesser known rowdies of the area. Besides Elumalai was literally the uncrowned monarch of liquor who freely indulged in rowdyism. To put down the antics of these elements some businessmen of the area belonging to Tuticorin and Tirunelveli brought one Radhakrishnan from Tuticorin. The clashes among these rowdies generally took place during night time. Soda bottles were freely used. In Vannarappettai there are number of workshops with lathes to make ever-silver (stainless steel) vessels. Here these groups also got their flashy patta swords and special Tirunelveli Palai sickles. In a matter of a few days Guru was murdered. In the next few months in the frequent clashes between Elumalai and Radhakrishnan groups three were hacked to death. Elumalai was an expert in Silambam (Wood fencing): once he escaped death from a murderer by using a towel as Silambam though he was inflicted with brutal injuries in one arm. After that Radhakrishnan and his brothers left this place, shifted their area of operation to ENNORE in Chengai District and established their illicitly brewed liquor empire there.

When cases pertaining to their clashes came up before the Hon'ble Madras High Court, I was working as A.C. in Vannarapettai (1980). On the way to Court and returning to their respective places Radhakrishnan's group used to throw soda water bottles over Elumalai's house which was near Royapuram overbridge: this was retaliated by Elumalai's group who threw stones at the buses where this group was travelling. Similarly whenever there used to be wrestling events in Kannappar Grounds, at the end of the bout, in Royapuram Kasi Medu area one could see soda water bottles flying like anything.

Bandobust arrangements would be strengthened. In the buses and in Royapuram over bridge sufficient policemen were posted to prevent both sides clashing. Once when they learnt that Tandiarpet police had gone home for taking meals, Radhakrishnan group attacked rowdy Siva in his house in G.A. Road. Siva was in a serious condition. When I learnt the news, I started from my residence situated within the premises of Veperi police station along with Inspector Kothandaraman and arranged for Siva to be sent to hospital in a police jeep. Not only that, the same night we arrested Radhakrishnan's group and locked them up in Tandiarpet police station. Around 10 P.M. the then Commissioner of Police phoned me up and said that an important political person in North Chennai wanted Radhakrishnan to be let on bail and that I should pacify him. Obeying his command, I went to the station. Inspector Mr.Kothandaraman was there. That politician was also there. I told the political person that these persons have been arrested under sections where bail is inapplicable and that he could move the court for bail when we produce them there on the following day. He said he would not leave the place till they were released. He stopped a cycle rickshaw which was going by that side and stationed himself opposite to the police station. I told the Inspector to close the gates of the station and remain inside and then left the place. After reaching home I phoned up the Inspector and asked him whether the politician was still there. He said that the politician left a while after I hade gone by the jeep. If police are very firm in our duty, we may earn the displeasure of the politician. But we can prove that law is inflexible.

19

Theft of Oil in Indian Oil Corporation Refinery

After completing three years of service in Coimbatore City as Dy.S.P. (Law & Order), in 1980 March I joined as Assistant Commissioner of Law and Order in Vannarapettai, Chennai. I then served under Mr.P.B. Rengasamy and Mr. Sripal. From Chennai Port crude oil is brought by pipeline to Korukupet-Tandiarpet oil depot near Tiruvotriyur border and then after refinement process petrol, naphtha, kerosene and black oil will be taken via Korukkupettai Oil Storage with huge pipes through the railway line and then sent to various places by lorry tankers and trains. Tiruvotriyur was under Chengai district jurisdiction.

In between Tiruvotriyur and Tandiarpet Oil Depot, there were thick thorny bushes (Kattu karuvai plants) and the pathway was used for illicit brewing of liquor. Black oil (furnace Oil) which is used as fuel will be stolen from the pipelines and used as fuel for fomenting liquor. This it became a big industry and the product sent to different places.

The oil line running from Tandiarpettai depot to Korukkupettai did not have iron fencing. A number of huts had come up in the area. After I took charge as A.C. in Vannarapettai one day the news came that there was fire in a colony in

6/3/93

Notorious criminal gives slip after attacking cop

Oil pilfering: 11 held

Madras, Mar 6: The police nabbed a notorious gang involved in pilfering oil and petrol from tankers in the city.

A police press release said, Rajendran alias Gate Rajendran of Thiruvottiyur an ex-detenu of Goondas Act, is indulging in the acts of dacoity and robbery in Madras city border. His victims were mostly drivers of oil tankers from IOC, Korukkupet. Under orders from the Commissioner of Police, Deputy Commissioner (Law and Order), A.P. Mohamed Ali formed a special party to curb the activities of this notorious criminal gang. Yesterday, during the busy evening hours this gang waylaid oil tankers. A police party rushed to the scene of crime. Gate Rajendran took to his heels off after assaulting a police constable attached to New Washermanpet police station. The constable sustained minor injuries.

Meanwhile, the police party accosted Jogire, Sandanam, Vinayagam and Bhoopalan, the prime associates of Gate Rajendran. On information furnished by them police arrested a gang consisting of Vijayakumar and six others while they were pilfering oil from lorry tankers. Oil drums and other equipment for pilfering oil from tankers all worth Rs 20,000 were seized by

Korukkuppettai. I left from my office to the spot and Inspector Mr.Govindan from Korukkupettai also had come to the spot. Fire engines had come, fire was put out.

Even though fire had been put out, I did not leave the place immediately. I wanted to investigate the reason for the break out of fire. And on investigation the shocking truth surfaced. I came to know that some gang had cut a hole by drilling in the pipeline which was three feet in diameter, had regularly been stealing barrels of petrol and selling them illegally. Immediately an advisory group was formed consisting of Mr.Shanmugam, Manager, IOC, D.S.P. Ganesan of R.P.F., and some railway officials. We proceeded to take some swift actions. The huts along the railway lines were removed; a road constructed for use of patrol vehicle. It was also decided to have fencing of the pipe line. The General Manager in Bombay of IOC, Mr.Ketaraman inspected the arrangements and complimented the efforts of Chennai Police.

However, still one could see even now huts have sprung up near the highway and are used to steal oil from lorry tankers proceeding from depot to various places.

20

Magnanimity of Bharat Ratna M.G.R.

All news papers carried sensational news in March 2007 regarding the refusal of Opposition Leader Rabri Devi to give precedence to the car of Bihar Chief Minister Nistish Kumar. Mrs. Rabri Devi was former Chief Minister of Bihar and wife of Mr. Lalu Prasad Yadav, Union Railway Minister. Presently Mr. Nitish Kumar is the Chief Minister of Bihar. Generally Opposition Leader is given the status of a Cabinet Minister and enjoys all facilities like Government quarters, car, telephone and travel facilities. When Mr. Nitish Kumar came to return home by his car after the assembly proceedings were over, he found the portico occupied by Mrs. Rabri Devi who was in the car conversing with party members. The security officials of the Chief Minister requested her to give way for the Chief Minister's car. But Mrs. Rabri Devi and the government driver did not heed to the request. Mr. Nitish Kumar who was irritated at this returned to his chambers. Only after Mrs. Rabri Devi left in her car, could the Chief Minister leave the place in his car. The driver of Mrs. Rabri Devi's car was transferred and some other driver posted. After Mrs. Rabri Devi expressed displeasure over the new driver, the government re-posted the same old driver. Everybody knows this story.

A similar incidence took place in 1980 when Bharat Ratna M.G.R. was the Chief Minister. I was the A.C. Law & Order, of Vannarappettai at that time. During the se legislative assembly session I was entrusted with security work there. At that time the opposition party had "Trinity" of Mr. Durai Murugan, Mr. Subbu and Mr.Rahman Khan. Their participation made the sessions lively despite ideological clashes. One day after the proceedings of the assembly were over, M.G.R. came to board on his car. But Mr. Durai Murugan's car was placed in front of M.G.R.'s car. At that time Messrs. Durai Murugan, Subbu and Rahman also were coming. I approached Mr. Durai Murugan with whom I was friendly when in Presidency College and requested him to give precedence to M.G.R.'s car. Even though he was my college mate, he told me, "No. Let M.G.R.'s car go after mine. After all I am also an M.LA." Everybody knew that M.G.R. was responsible for the higher studies of Mr. Durai Murugan.

M.G.R. was watching the discussion Durai Murugan with me from near the car at the portico: he signalled me to let them go and broadly smiled. Durai Murugan and others on boarding the car showed 'bye' to M.G.R. He also responded smilingly by waving his hand. This was the democratic spirit in Tamil Nadu at that time. Today it is unfortunate and it is a rarity to find leaders of different political parties speaking even in a friendly manner. One cannot forget how an Adi Dravida leader and Union Minister Mr. Arunachalam was asked to get down from a plane which reflected lack of maturity on the part of bureaucracy. No body can forget this painful episode!

21

A Rare Building Razed to the Ground by Fire

In Anna Salai, Chennai a grand building with exquisite designs was adorning for several decades. It was none other than "Spencers".

In 1980-81 I was the Assistant Commissioner in Vannarappettai, Chennai. At that time the Commissioner was Mr. Sripal and Mr. Subbiah, the Deputy Commissioner.

Usually once in a week the Deputy Commissioner and I would take up night patrolling. One evening the Deputy Commissioner said, "Ali, we are told that some gambling activity is going in a building at Tandiarpettai where Maharani Theatre is located. Shall we raid the place with the Control-room Police there without informing the Inspector?" I said yes. As planned around 11.00 p.m. we took Police from control-room and raided the building in Tandiarpettai. A number of gamblers were captured and they were taken to Tandiarpettai Police station along with money they used and other articles. At that time wireless message from the control-room informed that the Commissioner has asked all the officers on night duty to report near Spencers at Anna Salai. The D.C. and I immediately went to Spencer's complex.

We were aghast at what we saw there. The Spencers was on fire and the roaring fire was gaining momentum from the second floor on wards devouring everything. The fire could not be put out by ordinary fire engines despite best efforts by fire fighting men and police. The Commissioner asked me to help control the fight by joining the fire fighting personnel. But the devastating fire had been swiftly spreading everywhere.

Thereafter, it was decided to use "Snorkels ladder", new fire-fighting equipment which was untested so far. This is useful for operations to put out fire in high-rise buildings. It has facilities to use hydraulic pressure and pour water at great speed. It was pressed into service. The Commissioner asked me also to help the fire fighters. I too took up my position in the ladder. The ladder was lifted to a height of nearly 40 feet from the ground floor. Water was sprayed with great force and gradually the fire was brought under control, preventing its spread to many interior parts of the building. But the main wooden complex in the building, a number of electric, electronic appliances were completely burnt. The building looked like a skeleton of its own. The reconstruction and beauty of the present structure which has come there has made it a beautiful landmark. The present structure can be compared to its grandeur with some of the best buildings in places like Singapore. Still whenever I pass by this place, the memory of the old graceful building flits by like a nostalgic wave.

22

The Hand that Feeds-A Meeting with MGR in Delhi

When I was serving as Assistant Commissioner Chennai during 1980, I was sent to Delhi for getting training in intelligence wing in relation to security for VIPs. For the same training the Coimbatore Rural S.P. Mr. Arumugam also had been selected. Both of us along with our families were staying in the Tamil Nadu Special Guests House in New Delhi.

One day we got the information that the Chief Minister M.G.R. along with his wife Mrs. Janaki Ammal had been staying in the Tamilnadu House in New Delhi. Next morning, we decided that we must see him before proceeding to training and accordingly wore suits and went to the VIP room. We told he Security Officer Mr. Vivekananda Raju that we had come for special training and wanted to meet M.G.R. He said that the CM was with visitors who had come early in the morning and it may be difficult for us to see him. We requested him to explore the possibility of our meeting. He said he would try, went inside and then came back beaming and said the leader has asked us to come in.

M.G.R. was still in the bed wearing a lungi and a sleeveless banian and without the his famous white fur cap. He presented a picture of a noble hearted personality. At that time Tamilnadu Minister Mr. Muthusamy and Representative of Tamil Nadu at New Delhi Mr. Mohanarangam were seated in chairs. MGR got chairs for us and seated us and then arranged to give us coffee as well. He inquired as to why we had come to Delhi. We said we had come for getting special training for VIP protection. He wanted to know about the quality of food in Tamil Nadu house. We said the arrangements were good. He said that naturally as government officials, we would say so to please the CM. Then he asked about our children. I said I had three and Mr.Arumugam replied that he had none. Then he asked again that we should tell the truth about whether food is liked by our families and children. We stressed that we were getting good food and then only he was satisfied.

In 1982 the tender hearted MGR inaugurated nutritious noon meal scheme for school children in Tamukkam Grounds, Madurai. When he sat along with children, and when that hand that feed many also took the meal, I was Tallakulam D.S.P. If people called him affectionately as the hand that feeds, it was no exaggeration.

23

A Rare Audience with Indian Prime Minister, Annai Indira Gandhi

In 1980 when I was A.C. at Vannarapettai, Chennai I was sent to Delhi for a Training in Security to VIPs. Mr. Arumugam, Coimbatore Rural SP and I were in New Delhi for the same and this was an all-India scheme.

As part of the training we were taken to the Prime Minister's residence for viewing how the Prime Minister receives distinguished people in her house. The residence of the P.M. was in Akbar Road. In between the residence and the security camp office there was a wicket gate. The house was protected with high compound wall and there was barbed wire fencing as well. All vehicles and persons were permitted inside only after strict checking. Though we were Police Officials, we also were subjected to rigorous checking.

The IB officials were explaining to us the usual measures taken. At the other side of the great hall the Prime Minister was meeting a number of prominent people who had come from different parts of the country. When she came near us, she asked the security officer as to whom we were. He said that we had come for training. Immediately she asked us about the details of the training. Some officials requested her that we would be honoured to be photographed with her. She graciously smiled, agreed to it and posed with us for a photograph. Notwithstanding all the rigorous security measures when she was assassinated by her own bodyguards members of Khalistan extremist organisation, it was a permanent blot on the Police force.

In 1997 I was serving as A.I.G. in Coastal Protection Guard. At that time I had been to Delhi along with my family members. I took all the members of my family to the house where Annai Indira Gandhi had lived. I showed them the place we were photographed with her and the place where she was assassinated. The place was subsequently designed by using marbles as if still blood like water ran in the place. Yes, we could imagine in our mind's eye how Annai Indira had dedicated herself for the unity of the country and we felt her soul was something like the Heavenly Ganges.

24

Prostitution Put an End to in Central Lodge, Madurai Which Belonged to Madurai Devasthanam: Building Restored

I was working as Dy. S.P. in Tallakulam, Madurai during 1981-82. Opposite Central Theatre there was a building which had belonged to Madurai Temple Trust (Devasthanam). One Kurumbur Pandi was conducting Central Lodge there. He never used to pay rent regularly. Also there were complaints that the place was used for prostitution as well.

One night I sent an Inspector to check the lodge and find out what was happening. He visited the place and told me that nothing untoward was happening there. But I continued to receive complaints about undesirable activities there. So, with the assistance of Control Room constables, I raided the place. However, there were no traces of women having found there. Nor did I see any woman in any room. While getting down the steps from the terrace, there emanated anguished sounds from the wooden staircase. There were wooden planks. When I removed them I found two young girls were confined in that space. We asked them to come out of that cramped space. Then we checked all the rooms again. In one room there was a big monthly calendar. I tapped it and then found that it covered a niche and two girls were confined in that space with great difficulty! In fact one was sitting over the other. We lifted them out. On enquiry we learnt that the Central Lodge owner used to procure women from different places after some payment and used them for prostitution.

Whenever police raid took place, these girls were hidden in niches and small staircase space. I arrested the lodge owner Kurumbur Pandi and the four girls and sent them to the Court. The girls who had obtained bail by the evening had returned to the Central lodge itself. The same night we again raided the place. I was greatly surprised to find the lawyer who took them out in bail; one Arunagiri and the clerk of that Court with the files concerning the case were there with the girls. I arrested them all and sent them to the Court. I recommended that departmental action be taken against the Court Clerk. Afterwards he was suspended.

Thereafter as the building was used for purposes which would cause damage to public health, I saw to it that the same was restored to Devasthanam (temple trust) The authorities of Devasthanam thanked me profusely.

25

First Arrest Made by Me and Some Controversial Arrests Afterwards

After finishing training in Vellore Police Training College, on January 16th I was put for practical work in Madurai. In a few months time, Mrs.Indira Gandhi proclaimed Emergency throughout the country. Many opposition party leaders were arrested. In Tamil Nadu the DMK government was dismissed and many prominent leaders were arrested.

In south Tamil Nadu Mr. S.S. Thennarasu, affectionately called as 'King of Short-stories' and a highly cultured gentleman was at that time in Madurai: he was a heart patient and was in Padma Clinic near Meenakshi temple, undergoing treatment. I was given the responsibility to arrest him. I along with some Inspectors went to the hospital in the evening. I asked others to wait outside and went inside the patient's room. I was already acquainted with him. His wife was also helping him.

I was talking with Mr.Thennarasu about his health and the treatment he was undergoing. Accidentally when the door opened, he saw constables waiting outside and asked me whether I had come to arrest him. I said 'yes'. He said, "Wait for some time. I will get instructions from the doctor as to what food and medicines I must have while in jail." The doctor came and he got a list prepared and just got ready with a bed sheet and pillow and smiled, "Come on. Let's go." He could always be called a cultured person.

However, some of the arrests I made later on brought some controversies and embarrassments.

In 1977 I was serving as D.S.P. Coimbatore City, Law and Order. At that time Emergency had been lifted, elections had taken place and at the Centre a Janata party ministry under Mr. Morarji Desai had assumed power. In Tamil Nadu AIDMK captured power. Mrs. Indira Gandhi was arrested by the Janata Government. When that news came out, Coimbatore city congressmen had marched towards the District Collector's office in large numbers. They were arrested and then released after some time. Advocate Mr. R.S.Velan who always used to wear a white cap as MGR used to do, led a procession. While we arrested him and were about to take him in a police van, there was a melee and Mr. R.S.Velan fell down in the van. Next day he filed a case against me in a Court which was in near the Collector's office. Mr. Mayilsamy, a senior advocate appeared on my behalf. The case was on the file during all the three years when I was in Coimbatore City.

In 1980 I was transferred to Vannarapettai, Chennai as Assistant Commissioner. When I went to Coimbatore once in connection with the old case, Mr. R.S. Velan himself told my advocate Mr.Mayilsamy that he was withdrawing the case against me and also filed a petition to that effect. While I was leaving the Court, Mr.Velan took hold of my hands and told me that I should not bear any ill will as he had filed the case. Such a cultured act is truly typical of Coimbatore.

I was working as D.S.P. Tallakulam during 1982. Mr.Veeraraghavan was D.I.G. Madurai and Mr.Ganesan, S.P. Madurai Town and Mr. Chinnasamy D.S.P. Every 30th October there used to be celebration of Thevar Jayanthi (Freedom fighter and Thevar caste champion) in Madurai with a big procession. When the procession reached East Veli street, street lights would be switched off and people in the procession would be indulging in stone-throwing at the shops there. That year we had made elaborate security arrangements to prevent such occurrences. The same day a meeting had been organised by Human Rights Association at Karimedu to condemn state police. They had an idea to take out a procession on the following day. The constables informed us that they had spoken very badly about womenfolk of constables in that meeting. The policemen were much pained. There was a camp office meeting on 31st held by D.I.G. Mr.Veeraraghavan. Mr.Ganesan SP, D.S.P. Mr.Chinnasamy and I participated in it. The D.I.G. asked to see that the members of PUCL did not cross the limits.

The procession started from Kattabomman statue near Periar Bus Stand. Members of the PUCL began to gather for taking out the procession. City D.S.P. Mr. Chinnasamy and myelf were giving instructions to the constables regarding their duties. At that time the journalist-friend Mr. Hari was targeting the police and officials with his camera. We asked him to take photos of the procession and why should he take the photos of police. He said that it was his right and went on taking clicking the police. At that time they brought from the nearby RMS lane an effigy of a dog in which it was written 'Police'. That was brought to the fore.

They blocked the whole place near Kattabomman statue and prevented flow of traffic. Also raised slogans against the police. When I and Mr. Chinnasamy approached them and told them to take out the procession without obstructing the traffic, they pushed us about and indulged in arguments. Then we made a light lathi-charge, controlled the crowd and took to Sandaipettai Police Station.

We seated them on a bench in front of station writer's tale. When their names, place of origin and identification were verified we were shocked to find the name of former Bombay

High Court Judge Hon'ble Tarkunde, PUCL leader. We informed our higher authorities about this. Then we asked him to go to his place using police jeep. He refused to get into the police vehicle. Then we arranged for a taxi and sent him.

The next day's newspapers were full of news stating that there was lathi-charge on PUCL procession and Tarukunde's arrest, etc. The lawyers started an agitation. There was loud demand that I must be dismissed. However, MGR transferred me to Cuddalore and also ordered for a D.R.O. enquiry.

Similarly in 1980 when I was A.C. at Vannarapettai, a controversy arose when I arrested Mr. Rajasekaran, M.L.A. while he was blocking the Royapuram-Ennore road, Sivaji Ganesan threatened to go on fast unto death opposite the DGP office, unless I was suspended. But MG.R did not budge and stated that I had taken the correct stand. The above two are examples to show that MGR always stood for fairplay and justice and would never be a party to injustice.

26

1983 Tiruchendur Legislative Constituency By-Election-Recollection of Incidents Relating to It

After Mr.Subramania Pillai, an employee of Tiruchendur Murugan temple in Tuticorin district met with a mysterious death, Mr. Arumuga Adithan, M.L.A. who was suspected to have had a hand in his death, had also died in a car accident. A by-elction was ordered to be held in the constituency. At that time I was appointed as Dy. S.P. of Srivaikuntam. Mr. Shyam Sunder was the S.P. of Tuticorin district, Mr. Raj Mohan was the D.I.G. of Tirunelveli, Mr. Nirmal Singh Hira was the District Collector and Mr. Anbu Raj was the R.D.O. In the ensuing election, besides D.M.K. and A.I.D.M.K. other parties had also announced their candidates. To win the elections became a prestige issue for the D.M.K. and the A.I.D.M.K. The D.M.K. had made allegations that the death of Subramania Pillai and the disappearance of Vairavel (Diamond sword) were due to the then H.R. & C.E. Minister Mr. Rm.Veerappan and the M.L.A. Mr. Arumuga Adithan. Kalaignar M. Karunanidhi, had undertaken a 'padayatra' (roadwalk) from Madurai to Tiruchendur in 1982. M.G.R. was keen on somehow winning the by-election and for the first time asked Selvi Jayalalitha to undertake election propaganda work. Kalaignar said Selvi Jayalalitha was just reading out like a parrot the speeches written by the progressive writer Solai. However, people later on came to know that she had great talent for making speeches for any length of time without even notes in the hand while addressing legislative assembly sessions.

During the fiery propaganda of the election times, the Congress candidate Mr.Chandrasekar was introduced in Udankudi. Mr.T.P. Kosalram, M.P. gave a thunderous speech. I and S.P. had been overseeing the security arrangements and then were seated in the respective jeeps. Mr.Kosalram said, "A new Dy. S.P. has taken charge here. I hear that when the Human Rights Movement leader Mr. Tarkunde was addressing a meeting and condemning the police, this Dy. S.P. had lathi charged the procession. I would like to warn him. If he does anything like that to favour the ruling party, we would cut his tail." He had never seen me before that. When he got down from the stage, I went to him, introduced myself and said the Police had been functioning only impartially. This took place in the presence of all Congressmen. Mr. Kosalram said, "Sorry, I have not seen you before. When I see you, I have changed the wrong impression I had about you." After he left the place, S.P. Mr. Shyam Sunder shook my hands and said, "At the right time you had given an explanation to Mr. Kosalram" and appreciated me. It was something like bearding the lion in its own den!

27

Honesty of a Singapore Taxi Driver

During 1983 I had an incident admiring the honesty of a taxi driver at Singapore.

My Dad, A. Peer Mohamed and youngest brother, Umar were having a provision shop in the super market at Petaling Jaya, 5 K.M. away from Kuala Lumpur, the capital of Malaysia. I was D.S.P Srivaikuntam. The marriage of my brother, Umar, was fixed at Malaysia in July, 1983. I took leave and proceeded to Malaysia along with my wife and 4 children. After spending a month at Malaysia, we came to Singapore and stayed at the residence of my New college mate, Salih Marican, who was doing business there. We had enjoyed the sight seing at Santosa island by going in cable car and Tiger palm garden amusement park.

Two Days prior to our travel back to India, I want to reconfirm our tickets and then go for shopping. I had taken a pouch containing the passports, tickets and two thousand Malaysian currencies worth draft. My family and my friend, Salih Marican, took a taxi, from the flat, at 9 am to the complex where the re-confirmation of Singapore Airlines had to be done. It was a distance of 10 K.M. We got down near the Airlines complex and sent back the taxi. When we stepped into the Airlines office, then we came to know that we forgot to take the pouch containing the valuables. We were stunned and didn't know what to do. We were worried that we have not only lost the Malaysian draft but also our passport and tickets. We thought that we were going to be stranded there. We had not noted the number of the taxi also

Immediately my friend alerted the police by phoning up. In turn the police alerted the taxi control to inform all taxi drivers running in Singapore to check for the missing pouch. The formalities took an hour. The taxi driver with whom we traveled after dropping us took another passenger and traveled to a distance of 5 km. Then he took the second customer, a Chinese, who noticed the pouch lying on the back sheet. After dropping the second customer at a distance of 2 km, the taxi driver came back to the complex where we were waiting. In the meantime he had also heard the radio broadcast of the taxi control of the missing pouch. The taxi driver spotted us in the airline office and to our surprised handed over the pouch. He requested us to check the contents. I opened the pouch and found every item was correct. Our faces flushed with smiles. We thanked the driver profusely. My classmate handed over 10 Singapore dollars to the taxi driver. To our surprise the driver politely refused to accept. After waving his hand he sped of his taxi.

The whole incident reminded me of one thing, that is, why Singapore remains top tourist spot among Indians, because of the honesty among the public carriers, spike and span roads, public entertainments, cheap shoppings, so on.

28

Incident of Stone-Throwing at the Vehicle of M.G.R.

While M.G.R. was making election propaganda tour, it was arranged to have a meeting at Kayalpattinam, a predominantly Muslim area, in the night hours. Sultan Hajiar's house was selected as the place where he would have his dinner and rest. As Kayal Maulana had suggested that before public meeting MGR could meet Kayalpattinam people, this was accepted and without any prior announcement he got into his vehicle and started. However in a place nearby a meeting of D.M.K. was in progress. Leaders like Mr. Abdus Samad, Muslim League, Smt. Subbulakhsmi Jegadeesan of D.M.K. were the speakers there. On seeing the vehicle of M.G.R. some members of D.M.K. were agitated and threw stones at it. Learning that he was not on the right road, M.G.R. asked the driver to reverse the vehicle. It was then that the Security Officer Mr. Ramanathan understood that they had taken a wrong route. At that time D.I.G. Mr. Rajmohan, S.P. Shyam Sunder and I were at the D.M.K. meeting place. We learnt that on learning that M.G.R.'s vehicle had been stoned at, AIADMK volunteers were proceeding with weapons in ten vehicles from Tirunelveli and immediately cautioned Seythunganallur Sub-Inspector and stopped all the vehicles.

When AIADMK meeting began the party men were highly agitated. Kayalpattinam has a large Muslim population. Men folk often go to foreign lands and other parts of India on business. In order that no harm comes to womenfolk there, Keelakkarai industrialist Mr. P.S. Abdul Rahman got onto the stage and profusely apologised to M.G.R. for the stone-throwing incident. He exhorted that peace should prevail. M.G.R. responded suitably by appealing to people that protection of Muslims must be paramount concern for everybody and that AIADMK party men should not indulge in any retaliatory activities. His words brought great solace to everyone and restored peace.

29

Quick-Witted Response of Sivaji Ganesan

It had been announced that M.G.R. would be visiting a coastal village in Tuticorin district by name Punnakkayal by mid-day. A police unit for security purposes had already been despatched there under an Inspector, Mr. Nagalingam and S.I. Mr. Krishnan Nair. When we learnt that M.G.R. had left the Guest House of Tirunelveli Talaiyuthu Cements, myself, trainee A.S.P.s Mr. Subramanian, Mr. Radhakrishnan and Mr. Sekar left by car from Kayalpattinam to Punnakkayal. I asked the Sub-Inspector through wireless if he had attended to security work in Punnakkayal. He replied that he was there only attending to work. We had reached Punnakkayal by the time M.G.R. had reached Srivaikuntam. What we saw there shocked us. Sivaji Ganesan, a famous cine legend had reached that place and M.G.R. fans were surrounding his vehicle agitated. Along with Sivaji, Mr. Rajasekaran, President of Sivaji Ganesan Fans' association was also there. I told him that they had not asked for permission to address a meeting there and that permission had been given for M.G.R. to address a gathering. Sivaji Ganesan's fans were adamant and shouted that he should speak. I requested Sivaji Ganesan to proceed into the town and that there would be proper protection. Without addressing the meeting, Sivaji proceeded into the town with our protection, was there for a few minutes and left the place so that M.G.R. could address the meeting without any obstruction or problem. Thereafter M.G.R.'s vehicle had come with suitable security. As there was a breach of security the Inspector and Sub-Inspector were suspended.

30

Unfair Practices During the Counting of Votes

The counting of votes of By-elections of 1983 took place at Tiruchendur Taluk Office. Mr. R. Karuppanan, I.A.S. (Retd.) was the Observer, R.D.O. Mr. Anburaj was the Election Offcer and Mr.Sivakaminathan was the A.R.O. The Police Station was only nearby the Tahsildar's office. There was also a separate Election Control room. The D.I.G. Mr. Rajmohan, S.P. Mr. Shyamsundar, and SP of Tirunelveli Mr.R.V. Gopalan were all assembled there. At the place where votes were counted were Mr. K.P. Kandaswamy of D.M.K., Mr. Nellai Nedumaran and Mr. Sakthi Kothandam.

Counting began in the morning and lasted till late into the night. In the first round of counting D.M.K. had polled more votes in the coastal places: thereafter AIADMK began to take lead. Around 9 O'clock, counting was stopped for a while and everyone left for taking food. In those days the agents of political parties used to be permitted to go out for attending to urgent work. The Election Observer and R.D.O. were taking food in Tashildar's room. Usually after the counting of votes, the bundles would be placed in a room. At that time two bundles was pushed towards the table of party agents and hurriedly they were hidden. There was commotion and the matter was brought to the attention of the Election Observer. The R.D.O. and Tashildar asked the agents to return the bundle of votes. But they stated that there were no stacks of votes with them and at the same time managed to hide small bundles under the dhotis and saris. R.D.O. and Tashildar appealed to the D.I.G. to get back these bundles of votes. Under his instructions I and A.S.P. Ganesan asked those agents to return the votes without any fuss. But they hid them and claimed that there were no bundles of votes. I saw that there were two bundles under the table. I asked Tashildar Sivakaminathan to gather them and he took charge of one bundle. But Sakthi Kothandam of DMK took the other bundle and passed it on to one Karuppasamy of Sathankulam DMK and asked him to run away. I tried to follow him and in between some people as a group tried to prevent me and in the scuffle some buttons of my uniform also came off. I shook them off and caught hold of Karuppusamy, got the bundle and entrusted it to Tashildar. There was a CBCID enquiry regarding this and a case filed in Tiruchendur Court. But after the case was conducted and when judgment was to be delivered, due to change in the Government, the case was withdrawn.

31

Cuddalore Collector Directly Involves Himself in the Raids on Illicit Brewing of Liquor

During 1985-86 I was serving as Addl. Dy. S.P. (Prohibition) of South Arcot (Cuddalore-Villupuram districts). Even though Prohibition was in force in South Arcot, as that was not the case in Pondichery and as there was a number of sugar-cane crushing factories in the place, raw materials for brewing liquor were easily available in the area. It had almost got the status of cottage industry here. After I took charge of the post, I arrested a number of people who were indulging in illicit brewing and put them in prison under the Goonda Act.

Adjacent to Old Cuddalore is a place called Panangattu colony. The place was lying adjacent to the coast. The place is full of thorny bush. This was very convenient for brewing illicit liquor. Because of the difficult terrain, it was also an ideal place for storing the liquor. Even though frequent raids were conducted and pots and vessels used for brewing were broken, and male offenders arrested, still the practice was carried on by women folk. Young children were used as help by these women. Whenever a police jeep was sighted, women folk would rush back to their huts and young boys would be looking after the ovens. Everybody knew that boys would not be arrested. These became something like a hide and seek game and it became difficult to wipe out this practice of illicit brewing. I decided that something serious must be done and recommended to the Collector, Mr. R.C. Banda I.A.S that two leading women offenders must be arrested under the Goonda act, 1982 for illicit brewing of arrack.

He wanted clarification from the S.P. Mr. Radakrishna Raja, I.P.S. as to how women could be arrested under the Goonda act. The S.P. told me about the doubts of the Collector.

I met the Collector and explained how in this Panangattu Colony men and women put up young children in the front and freely indulge in brewing liquor. I also explained that as the place is so nearby Cuddalore, the whole officialdom gets a bad name and therefore strict action was necessary. He asked me to come to his camp office in the afternoon. I thought he would sign the papers on my recommendation of arresting women and accordingly went to the Collector's camp office in the afternoon. To my surprise he said, "Shall we now go to Panangattu Colony? Only when my conscience is satisfied that women do indulge in this, would I sign in the orders under Goonda Act." After 2.00 p.m. we left in his car and proceeded to Panangattu colony. Women folk were using big pots and one could see many women busy with ovens and brewing the liquor. The moment they saw our vehicle they rushed back to their huts and sat quietly there. Only children were just casually looking at the pots and ovens. The Collector himself took up a long stick and broke all the pots and put off fire in the ovens. He was fully satisfied with the role of women. Accordingly he signed as recommended by me in the orders for the arrest of women under the Goonda Act.

32

Sri Lanka Tamil Liberation Telo Camp Surrounded

Organisations like LTTE, TELO, IROS, PLOTE and EPRLF formed their cadre of militants and gave them training and were conducting a number of violent activities in Sri Lanka. They were also getting help from political parties in Tamil Nadu. It is to be noted that at that time the Indian Government tacitly supported the struggle and provided arms and ammunitions between 1981-84. They had established camps in Tamil Nadu But the rivalries between the groups of Militant organisations took a violent turn of annihilating their leaders one after other not only in Srilanka, like Srisabarathinam and Mathaihyan but also like EROS Padmanabha in Tamilnadu. It resulted in the killing among fraternities.The results of the armed culture could be seen subsequently in the exchange of fire between LTTE leader Prabhakaran and PLOTE leader Umamaheswaran in Pondy Bazaar, a busy commercial locality in Chennai, a bomb blast in Meenambakkam International Air-Port which claimed more than 30 lives, machine guns being freely used in many places in Tamil Nadu, the use of hand-grenades and similar extremist activities. With great humanitarian gesture M.G.R. donated Rupees 3 crores (government money) to LTTE. When

Dr. Kalaignar M. Karunanidhi, opposition leader offered the money collected on his birth day to LTTE, the latter refused to take the same. At one stage the activities of these militants went beyond limits and it was decided by a high-level committee to capture their arms, wireless equipment etc. and scrutinise their numbers in Tamil Nadu.

At that time, in 1986, I was functioning as S.P. in Salem District. The D.G.P. there was Mr. K.Ravindran, Mr. Mohandas CID, DGP, Mr. Sripal I.G. (Law & Order). Mr. Mohandas, CID, DGP ordered that a camp of TELO militants in Kollimalai and LTTE office which was functioning in a house at Chevvaipet should be surrounded and all the arms confiscated. D.I.G. Mr.Neilwal ordered that TELO armed camp must be surprised under my direction.

We left Salem in the early morning by 3.00 a.m. reached Kollimalai hills around 5.00 a.m. and from there proceeded to Servarayan hill temple. Thereafter by foot we proceeded in the mountain area. At the end of a two km journey, there was a check-post. A TELO militant was there with hand grenade. We asked him to show the path towards TELO camp. After about 5 km journey we saw two TELO militants sitting on tree tops with machine guns as watchers on surveillance duty. In the thick forest areas we saw the armed camp of the militants surrounded by three hillocks: on the top of one of hillock, the words, "TELO Armed Camp" became visible: pebbles had been used to draw the words.

The ground had been levelled and a round shaped training place had been formed. Tight-rope walking and overcoming obstacles were the activities. We also saw many bunkers, the commander's room, doctor's room, an underground arsenal, a first-aid camp, a kitchen, dining hall and were surprised. We asked all militants to be assembled. Their arms, instruments of wireless communications etc. were taken by us. We asked them as to how many days had elapsed since they had taken good food after seeing their poor physique.. They said due to acute financial difficulties they had not had good meal for the last fifteen days. We handed over to their leader some money to them from the funds we had brought. As Deeepavali was approaching, we asked them to have sumptuous feast. In a letter written on 11.11.1986, DGP Mr.Ravindran warmly appreciated the horripilate deed done by us: "You and your constables carried out a very difficult job without any untoward happening in a very magnificent manner. My compliments to you!"

33

Unforseen Backlash for Undertaking a Humanitarian Work

In June 1987 I took charge as the Commandant of Special Police Forces in Palani. The TSP camp and their families apartments were situated about six km. from Palani on the Dharapuram road. The colonies got water through pipe from the foothills of Palani. During 1987 there was severe shortage of water all over the place.

We had made a new tennis ground inside Palani camp. We also invited the Municipal Commissioner of Palani for tennis game. One day I requested him to arrange for one lorry of water supply to our colony. He, too, had made arrangements for the supply of water. In 1988 January I met the District Collector of Dindigul, Mr. Sarangi and explained to him the difficulties faced by us in the colony for water. I also requested him to come and play in our tennis ground. On 28.1.1988 he came to Palani Camp, played a game of tennis and went round the place. At that time the women folk also represented to him about the acute shortage of water. He promised that he would do the needful. He sent the B.D.O. of Oddanchatram and officials of TWAD to this camp to explore the possibility of digging bore wells. As it was a rocky terrain, they were unable to locate the springs. I conveyed this information to the Collector. He got in touch with a foreign priest, Mr. James Kimpton who was running a service organisation called "Reach the Unreached" at Genguvarpatti near Vattalagundu and asked for advice in this matter. Mr. Kimpton told the Collector that he would do the needful and then came to Palani Camp with his assistants. He searched the area for suitable springs, found out five places where bore wells could be dug and arranged for the execution of the plan. In fact after the needs of the families of colony were met, surplus water was utilised for raising Sun-flower plants. Mr. Jaffer Ali, who was the D.I.G. of Armed Forces at that time, had mentioned this with appreciation in the annual report for that year.

During 1988 President's Rule, I was posted as S.P. of Dharmapuri district. On 13.7.1988, Mr.Shyam Sunder who was my successor in Palani had written a letter to D.G.P. to accord sanction for 5 deep bore wells drilled. However, the D.I.G. Armed Reserve Force, Tiruchi was directed to issue charge memo to me as to how without the permission of higher authorities these bore wells were dug. Accordingly I received P.R.4/89 Charge memo. About that time procedures were initiated to promote state police officials to I.P.S. rank. I was, therefore, shocked to receive the charge-memo. I immediately contacted Mr. Sarangi who was the Collector of Dindigul at that time and also his successor Mr.Sakti Gandhidas. By their letters dt.2.12.1989, 11.12.1989 they had stated that five wells were dug only on their sanctioning the same. The I.G. of Armed Reserve at that time, Mr. Dewaram took me with those letters to D.G.P. Mr. Dorai and acquainted him with the matter of charge-memo. Mr.Dorai expressed surprise that instead of appreciating the efforts made to relieve the sufferings due to water shortage, why someone had issued a charge memo. On March 6, 1980 issued orders cancelling the charge memo. After this incident, for some time, there was a set back in young officers implementing welfare measures for the families of constables.

34

Prime Minister Rajiv Gandhi's Tamil Nadu Tour – My Escort Duties

When I was functioning as Deputy Commissioner (Law & Order) in Chennai North, the night of May 21, 1991 turned out to be the most unforgettable one.

In 1988 I was working as S.P. of Dharmapuri district. At that time President's rule had been imposed in Tamil Nadu. As Assembly elections were due in Tamil Nadu, Rajiv Gandhi undertook a lightning tour visiting many villages. I and the present I.G. Mr. Subramaniam were then appointed as Escort officers for Rajiv Gandhi. My journey with him started from Krishnagiri. After getting down from the helicopter Rajiv himself drove the jeep effortlessly through the country roads which greatly surprised me. Everywhere people thronged to give him a hearty welcome. On the way to EX. Central Minister Mr. Mohan Kumaramangalam's house in Tiruchengode he stopped his jeep in front of a hut and went inside. The woman inside was simply stupefied to see him. She offered him a tumbler of water soaked in cooked rice. He drank it with great relish. This incident showed his great affection for the poor.

In the vehicle in which Rajiv was travelling, former Central Minister Mr. Arunachalam also was together when Tirunelveli and Virudhunagar districts were toured. After touring several districts, he returned to Sankar Cements Guest House in Virudhunagar around 1 O'clock in the night. Despite that he resumed his tour by 6.00 a.m. in the morning. He was very fresh in the morning and his face shone like a fresh lotus flower. While crossing through Rajapalayam, about midday, he got down from the vehicle and accepted shawls and garlands from the public. In some places he tasted the tender coconut offered by the people. A Special Protection Group formed a ring around him. At one stage he stopped at many places in the route and heard from people about their grievances. The Union Minister Mr. Arunachalam, too, had to be outside this protective ring. When he attempted to translate what the people told from Tamil to English by going near him, the central security people stopped him.

I went and told them that Mr.Arunachalam was a Union Minister. But an official there said that they were just doing their duty. When such was the case when he was in power, it was very tragic that when he was not in power, the Central ministry under Mr.Chandrasekar which came to power with the help of Congress of which Rajiv was the leader could not give sufficient protection and on May 21, 1991 he became a victim to the conspiracy of the Srilankan terrorists at Sriperumbudur. Had he been alive today he would have transformed India into a powerful force in the world equal to U.S. Not only that, he would never have permitted the demolition of Babri Masjid, and the genocide of Muslims in Gujarat which violated the sovereignty of our country. This is the truth.

When travelling between Kurmbur and Arumuganeri in Tuticorin district, Rajive Gandhi watched women folk transplanting paddy in the fields. He stopped his Maruthi Jonga Jeep and got down. The women, who were transplanting the paddy, came running to the road and were surprised to see him. Mr. Moopanar, Tamilnadu Congress President nearby Rajiv. Rajiv told Moopanar in English to ask those women who he was. Moopanar asked them, "Do you know who this is?" At one voice they replied, "Oh!mom! This great man (maharajan) Rajiv, is he not Indira Gandhi's son?" Rajiv wanted to know what they replied. Moopanar said that they told that he was Indira Gandhi's son. Rajiv laughed. Then he told Moopanar. "They identify me better as Indira Gandhi's son rather than the Prime Minister of India." Then he continued his Tirunelveli and Kanyakumari district tour, had his dinner at Marthandam at 11.00 p.m. and reached Trivandrum airport. It was one a.m. then. He took leave of DGP Mr. P.B. Rangasamy and IG Mr. Raghavan with a smile. I was a little away. My rank was S.P. But he called me by my name, shook hands with me and said, "Good night". This incident is still fresh in my mind. It was my misfortune that I was on duty as Deputy Commissioner in Chennai when this lotus faced Rajiv was cruelly decimated due to terrorist ploy of Srilankan tamil human-bomb who came in the pretext of a refugee at Sriperumbudur.

35

1989 State Legislative Assembly Elections-Boycott Agitation by Vanniars

In December 1987 M.G.R. passed away and political instability led to President's rule in Tamil Nadu. At that time I was the Commander of Special Armed Reserve Police in Palani. An All India Congress General conference was held at Maraimalai Nagar, Chennai. The then Prime Minister Rajiv Gandhi attended the sessions and stayed there for three days. I was entrusted with security arrangements. The then D.G.P. P.B. Rangasamy appreciated my services, recommended and appointed me as Superintendent of Police, Dharmapuri District. Mr. Alexander took over as the D.I.G. Vellore.

As elections were shortly due in Tamil Nadu, the Prime Minister Rajiv Gandhi had whirlwind tour. Twice I was appointed as his Escort Officer. Elections were announced during 1989 January. All important political parties separately contested. Vanniar Sangham led by Mr. Ramadoss had made an announcement that it was boycotting the elections. In places like Villupuram, Cuddalore, Salem, Dharmapuri etc. where there were large number of Vanniars restlessness prevailed;

vehicles were torched. Shady trees on either side of the road were cut and road blocks formed to prevent free flow of traffic. Police who went to prevent such atrocities were attacked by Vanniar association. In the affected districts along with Tamil Nadu Special Armed forces, Central Reserve forces were also involved in maintaining law and order.

In the battlefields, vehicles used to be destroyed by flinging at them magazine powder known as 'claymore'. In Dharmapuri bombs were hidden inside cow dung which would explode when the wheels run over them, leading to accidents. Also there was the practice of burning the trees by pouring kerosene or petrol in the big holes on the trees and lighting them. The trees would burn and then fall on the side obstructing the traffic. Vellore D.I.G. Mr.Alexander and I worked tirelessly day and night: arrested miscreants and arranged for highways patrolling.

The President of Vanniar Association, Mr. Subramaniam, a former I.A.S. officer, met me and protested against the arrests. I told him how members of their association had indulged in acts of vandalism and he could see them for himself and then state what we had done was right or wrong. After some time he phoned up and said that he met me based on wrong information and that our actions were quite right. Similarly Mr.Ilaya Perumal, leader of Adi Dravidars met me and requested that due protection must be given to people of his community; this was also done.

Arrangements had been made to despatch materials required for setting of election booths at Eriyur and Neruppur villages in Pennagaram taluk, at the point of confluence of Cauvery. Vehicles left the place taking along with them constables and officials and departed for hilly areas. But an important bridge on our way had been blasted. We repaired it, proceeded to two villages, set up voting booths, police control rooms etc. On our return we found the bridge had been blown off again using magazine powder. Then we arranged for patrolling the area with a vehicle, repaired the bridge again.

Still on the night preceding the Election Day when constables were sleeping, efforts were made to blast the building. Fortunately only the front door steps were damaged.

Such hard work was greatly appreciated by D.I.G. Mr.Alexander in my annual report on 18.7.1989 with these words: "This officer maintained Law & order duties very efficiently. The way he handled Vanniar agitation and performed security work for the Prime Minister twice are commendable."

36

1991 May 21: A Nerve Racking Night!

A few months before the assassination, Rajiv Gandhi had participated in a function at Kamaraj Arangam, Teynempet, Chennai. He was not in power then. As the Deputy Commissioner of North Chennai, I was responsible for security arrangements and was on the stage. When he saw the overflowing crowd, Rajiv became very exuberant and despite scorching sun rushed to the podium with great agility. It is not an exaggeration if we have to say that May 21, 1991 was black letters day in Tamil Nadu. Tamil Nadu which had showered prosperity on those who had sought refuge here witnessed the tragedy of a great son of the country falling prey to the assassination by Sri Lanka extremists. If it happened to any one of the former Presidents of America, it would have waged a full scale war and wiped out the entire LTTE militant outfit from Srilanka. But Indians are naturally peace loving and bore the brunt of Srilankan refugees' treachery patiently.

I had sent my government vehicle Ambassador 8181 for some minor repairs to workshop on May 21, 1991. As there was no alternative government vehicle, I was provided with a taxi. After the duty was over, I got down at the residence in Vepery, told the taxi driver to finish his food and then sleep at Veperi Police Station. Exactly by 10.30 in the night, from Chennai City Control Room, Sub-Inspector Poongavanam rang me up and said, "Sir, There seems to have been a severe bomb blast in Sriperumbudur where Rajiv had participated in a meeting. There were intense activities in St.Thoms control room. There is a possibility of many to be brought to hospitals here." Immediately I phoned up to Vepery Police Statation and asked the Taxi to come to my house. I then contacted the Deans of Government Hospital, Keelpalk Hospital and Stanley Hospital and told them to be ready for emergency measures. I asked Harbour Asst.Commissioner Mr.Subbarayan and Inspector Gopalakrishnan to come near Government Hospital opposite Central Railway Station. I also hastened there. In the Control Room Van only fewer policemen were there. Besides, there were hospital R.M.O. Mr. Pir Mohammed, Casualty Doctors Mr. Raja and Ms. Poongothai. At the main entrance we stationed the sentry and three of us waited.

By about 11.00 P.M. an old ambulance with just violet overhead lamp entered the hospital and proceeded towards casualty section. Lights were switched on inside the ambulance. Inside were Mr. Moopanar, Mr. Vazhapadi, Delhi journalist Suman Dubey and Mrs. Jayanti Natarajan. As Vazahapadi was familiar with me, he cried at seeing me and said, "Ali Sir, our leader is gone! Please bring stretcher." I, A.C. and Inspector brought a mobile stretcher from the casualty section. The whole of left side of handsome Rajiv from head to foot was blown up and full of blood. Even I was horrified at the sight. Then we recovered ourselves and placed the body in the stretcher in the casualty doctor's room, locked it and directed Mr.Gopalakrishnan to guard the place. Then we came out to attend to security work.

At that time Commissioner Rajasekaran called me in the mike, "Ali, some injured from Sriperumbudur will be coming to the hospital. Arrange for security." I told him, "Sir, the dead

The nerve-racking hours

MADRAS

The few hours between the death of Rajiv Gandhi in an explosion in Sriperumbudur on the night of May 21 and the sending of his body by a special aircraft to Delhi the next morning were nerve-racking for the police.

Immediately after the ghastly incident, information trickled in at the city police control room that there had been a blast at Sriperumbudur and some of the injured would be brought here. On receipt of this message, the Deputy Commissioner of Police, Law and Order (North), Mr. A. P. Mohamed Ali, alerted the Government hospitals to keep them in a state of preparedness. Since the van carrying the body of the former Prime Minister did not have a wireless set, the police here could not be informed of its destination. This necessitated sending of police vehicles fitted with mikes to find out the van's location.

Only after the arrival of the body of Rajiv Gandhi at the General Hospital here did the police come to know the magnitude of the disaster. [...] this time the news about the killing had spre[ad] fast and tension was building up in the city a[nd] other places. With only a limited number of p[o]lice personnel available at hand, a good numb[er] being involved in patrolling and bandobust d[uti]es, the first task of the police was to prevent t[he] surging public from coming anywhere near t[he] hospital. The police vehicles came in handy f[or] blocking the entry to the EVR Periyar Salai fro[m] the junctions of Muthusamy Bridge, Wallax Ro[ad] and Central Station.

Soon a posse of policemen was posted [in] front of the hospital as a precautionary measu[re].

First the police requested the Director [of] Medical Education to come over to the hospit[al] to muster more number of doctors. As he did n[ot] have a vehicle to travel at that hour, he wa[s] brought in a police patrol vehicle.

After shifting the body to the mortuary, the r[e]sponsibility increased and also tension. First [a] police vehicle had to be despatched to get th[e] doctor who should do the post-mortem. Simult[a]neously, a police inspector was asked to mak[e] arrangements for getting the coffin ready. Th[e] doctor who could do embalming of bodies live[d] at Tirumangalam and she had to be brought i[n] another police vehicle. However, that task wa[s] not performed here.

The post-mortem over, the cloth for covering the body and the National Flag (kept above the Congress flag) were brought by the police an[d] the vehicle carrying the body was later escorte[d] to the airport.

Even as these were going on, violence on a largescale had broken out at T.P. Chatram and Otteri.

K. T. Sangameswaran

Policemen keep watch at the gate of the General Hospital on the night of May 21

body of Mr. Rajiv has come." Mr. Vazhapadi asked me to take him to a telephone so that he could talk to the Govenor. I took him to casualty room. From the telephone exchange got a line for him. As he was a friend of the Governor Mr. Bhishma Narayan Singh, Vazhapadi told him, "Mr. Singh, come here. Our leader Rajiv is dead. We are in General Hospital." He was almost sobbing. Thereafter the Police Commissioner came with due security forces. "Those who are responsible for security have failed. The police have failed in its duty." Like that there were shouts. D.G.P. Mr. Rangasamy and I.G.

W. Dewaram had come by that time. Agitated congressmen and some anti-social elements tried to barge into the hospital. But the police at the entrance stopped many of them. Some gathered up stones and wooden blanks left there for construction work, tried to use them as missiles and began to shout at the higher authorities saying that they failed to give proper protection to Rajiv Gandhi and had thus killed him. With great difficulty they were controlled. Outside the hospital, some tried to get into Central Railway Station and tried to create disturbances. To drive them away forces were sent from the Control Room. After some time the Governor B.N. Singh arrived at the hospital. Then it was decided to send Rajiv's body to mortuary.

After a while, the injured S.P., at present ADGP, Nanjil Kumaran, a leader of the TNCC Mr. Kumaran and woman Sub-Inspector Arusuya were brought to hospital for treatment. A little later they were sent to Apollo Hospital. The control room learnt that not only in Chennai but in many parts of the state there were disturbances and road blocks.

Mr.Moopanar along with Suman Dubey, senior journalist from Delhi who had accompanied Rajiv came near to me and asked, "Sir, please find out where the body of Mr. Gupta, security officer of Rajiv –whether it is in Sriperumbudur or in hospital?" I got in touch with Chengai Control Room and asked for the details. They told that his body was in the place where the

Rajiv body is being taken by R.K. Dawan, PCC leader Ramamoorthi and others to the IAF flight at Meenampakkam airport, Chennai.

blast went off. Moopanar wanted to know whether the pistol was there with his body. I asked for the particular and they said the pistol was there. Thereafter they wanted his body and pistol to be safely brought to the hospital. I informed Chengai Control room accordingly.

Mr.Iqbal who was Police Superintendent from my native place was Kanchipuram District Superintendent of Police at that time: Sriperumbudur where the blast had taken place was under his jurisdiction. His younger brother and my class mate Nizam met me at 2.00 a.m. in the hospital and said, "Ali, I learn that my brother is dead. But I cannot go to Sriperumbudur. There are road blocks all over the place. I can go only when adequate security is given." He was also crying profusely. I apprised the Commissioner and gave him adequate security and sent him to Sriperumbudur.

We understood that the body of Rajiv must be taken to Delhi after a post-mortem and due process of mummification must be done. As the anatomy doctor familiar with that was in Anna Nagar a request was made to get a police van to bring him. I sent Doctors Raja and Poonkothai in my car and brought the anatomy doctor. There was no electricity in the anatomy block which was in one corner of the hospital. With the help of candles and torch lights we made arrangements for getting equipment for proper mummification and then went to mortuary.

Early in the next morning Sonia, the wife of Rajiv, children Rahul and Priyanca were all due to arrive in Chennai airport and we were told that they would thereafter come to hospital. But for security reasons the body was asked to be brought to the airport. Similarly Rajiv's security officer Mr.Gupta's body was asked to be brought to Chennai airport from Sriperumbudur. When I had duly taken care of security arrangements when Rajiv was Prime Minister, I found myself taking his decimated body to airport. I felt really very unfortunate on that account!

The body was taken to airport and through VIP lounge was placed in a room in the old building. Sonia and children and other congress leaders saw the body. Thereafter the body was taken in an Indian Air Force plane to Delhi. People like Vazhapadi and Dhwan also accompanied the body.

My particular services on that night were recounted to Jain Commission on Rajiv assassination by North Chennai Congress Leader Jyothi: the statement greatly appreciated my work.

37

Kidney Racket in a Prominent Hospital

In January 2007 the much talked about news was the people who were affected by Tsunami of 2004 were also victims of losing their kidneys! There are two kidneys in human body which enable proper functioning of the internal organs of the body. Even if one kidney is damaged, one can survive with the help of the other. Kidneys are damaged due to high sugar, jaundice and stress. Such affected people can get one kidney from close relatives and transplant it on their system and extend their life span. For example, the late Bharat Ratna M.G.R. got a kidney from his niece Leelavathi and continued to live for some more time. There was gradual awareness among kidney patients about getting alternative kidneys. At the same time the nefarious practice of unscrupulous people resorting to stealing others' kidneys also started.

In 1991, I was the Deputy Commissioner, Law and Order for Chennai North. At that time Mr. Manickam was Inspector of Kilpalk Police Station and Mr. Sundaramurthy was Assistant Commissioner of Pulianthope. A complaint was received that a railway assistant was offered but not given a huge amount for the kidney by someone in a prominent hospital situated in Poonamalle High Road under the jurisdiction of Kilpalk police

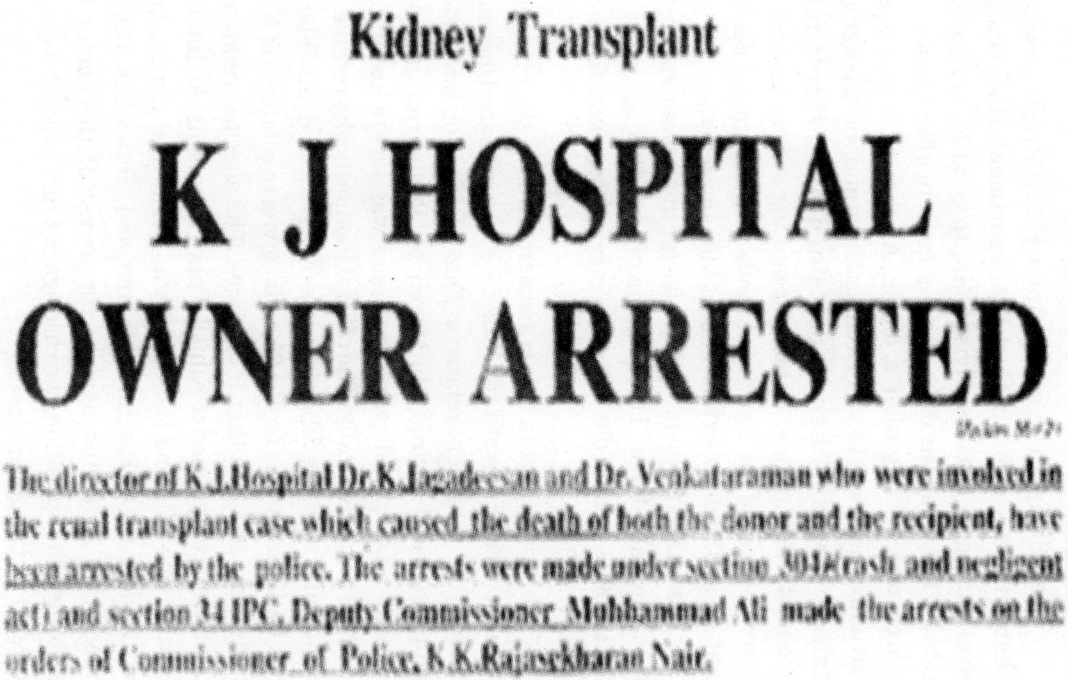

Kidney Transplant

K J HOSPITAL OWNER ARRESTED

The director of K J Hospital Dr. K. Jagadeesan and Dr. Venkataraman who were involved in the renal transplant case which caused the death of both the donor and the recipient, have been arrested by the police. The arrests were made under section 304 (rash and negligent act) and section 34 IPC. Deputy Commissioner Muhammad Ali made the arrests on the orders of Commissioner of Police, K.K. Rajasekharan Nair.

station. It was also complained that even the cheque given was forcibly taken back and then torn into pieces. At that time we had President's rule in Tamil Nadu. On enquiry, the following facts emerged.

One Sampath living in Anna Pillai Street, Sowcarpet, Chennai was working in Customs department. His kidney had been damaged. Doctors advised him to go in for transplanted kidney. His relations did not come forth to offer kidney. So a search was on to gather a donor. At that time one bachlor Ravindran who was in poor circumstances and was a lower grade Railway servant, kalasi, explained his difficult family circumstances to Ajeez Patcha for making arrangements of his sister because of the Paucity of funds. Ravindran did not know that Ajeez Patcha was a broker in kidney rackets.

Patcha took Ravindran to a doctor in a prominent hospital in Poonamalle Road. The customs official had agreed to give Rs. 25, 000 for the kidney and Ravindran was given an advance of Rs. 1, 000/-

The awful fact in this transaction was in the presence of Doctor. Official Sampath and Kalasi Ravindran signed documents stating that they were relatives. This falsification took place in the presence of doctors. On March 14, Ravindran underwent operation. On the following day there was severe loss of blood and he died pathetically. The official Sampath who received the kidney also died the following day. When he died, his relations took back the cheque for Rs. 25, 000/- given to relations of Kalasi Ravindran and tore that into pieces. The shocked relatives of Ravindran complained to Kilpalk Police about this. An intensive enquiry was held and the doctor who performed the operation and broker Ajeez Patcha were arrested. But when Doctors' association protested against the arrest of the doctor who performed the operation, the case against him was subsequently dropped by the government.

But even though Organ Transplantation Act was framed subsequently to prevent this kidney theft, still taking advantage of the poverty of people and using the hardships felt by Tsunami people in Chennai Ennore area and Komarapalayam near Salem they are cheated. Police and government must come forward and take severe action to prevent fraudulent practices. Then alone this menace of kidney racket would be brought under control.

Recently when the news came out that one Venkatalakshmi of Komarapalayam who was acting as wife of kidney donors, lost her chastity to brokers, the whole of Tamil Nadu could digest the news only with big shock and dismay.

38

North Chennai Election Duty and Appreciations Received

On 30th January, 1991 after the dismissal of DMK Government, I assumed charge as the Deputy Commissioner of North Chennai. Shortly before the elections were due in Tamil Nadu, on May 21, Rajiv was assassinated by LTTE at Sriperumbudur. Thereafter the elections which were earlier postponed were held on 15.6.1991. As elections came after postponement, it was thought that there would be chaos and strife; even the assistance of Army had been sought. But as Tamil Nadu Police force itself functioned with great sagacity and attended to election duties with deep commitment nothing untoward occurred anywhere in the state, particularly in North Chennai which was considered a haven for rowdies. My part in the maintenance of law and order during those difficult days was greatly appreciated by the then DGP (Law and Order) Mr. Dewaram in his letter of 19.6.1991. Madras City Commissioner Mr. K.K. Rajasekaran Nair wrote on 25.6.1991 in a letter to me, "I appreciate your excellent work. I trust your services will be even more glowing in future." Similar sentiments were expressed by DGP, Mr. B.P. Rengaswamy in his letter of 21.6.1991.

Acharappan Street in Kothawal Chavadi is often referred to as the grain market of North Tamil Nadu. Labourers who are generally in charge of moving goods through cart struck work on 18.7.1991. Members of Grain Merchants Association met me and requested to give suitable protection to them. I called the representatives of both the associations and conducted parleys. Also, made suitable security arrangements at Kothawal Chavadi. The timely action of the Police department and the protection given led to peaceful settlement of dispute. The strike came to an end. Our services were appreciated by Grain Merchants Association, who wrote on 25.7.1991. "We are very happy to have received due protection. We express our heartfelt gratitude."

39

VIP Protection – Gypsies (Narikkuravars) Mischief

In 1991 after AIADMK formed the ministry, Chief Minister Jayalalitha announced that she would meet people and receive petitions listing grievances. As there was threat perception from LTTE to her, additional security arrangements had been made. But when the day of her meeting the public came, a very big crowd, nearly 10,000 had assembled at the fort Secretariat.

From early in the morning people had been making a bee-line towards the fort. At that time there were no barricades. We were taking care of the security measures under Commissioner Mr. Rajagopalan and Chief Minister's Security Officer Mr. Vijayakmar. The crowd was so great that even our caps sometimes rolled on the ground. We were very much worried that there should not be any stampede leading to loss of lives. Fortunately nothing untoward happened. Thereafter it was decided that the Chief Minister would meet people from different districts on different days. Then adequate barricades, fencing etc. came into being. Also, food packets were given for the visitors.

When people from Chennai and Kanchipuram districts assembled, a very large number of narikkuravars had also come.

Usually men and women are permitted after separately frisking. In Sriperumbudur, Rajiv assassination as it was thought that woman-human bomb Dhanu was responsible for the tragedy, now it was decided to check women separately by women constables. Two narikkuravar women had kept two squirrels hidden in their blouses, which surprised us a great deal! Mr.Vijayakumar appreciated me and the women constables and gave some cash to the latter as reward.

40

Murder in Stanley Hospital during Night and Prompt Arrest of the Accused in the Night Itself

Kodungaiyur was formerly under the Chengalpattu District jurisdiction. One Subbiah, and his nephew Chera had formed a group and Vellai Ravi of Mahakavi Bharati Nagar had formed another group and were indulging in rowdyism. Both the group members were Burma repatriates. On the night of November 12, 1991 when Subbiah was going in his bike at Kodungaiyur over bridge, Vellai Ravi's rowdies threw chilly powder on Subbiah's eyes, attacked him with deadly weapons, assumed that he had been killed and fled from the scene. But luckily Subbiah was alive and was brought to Stanley Hospital. When doctors were examining him in the casualty ward, the news that he was alive had reached the assailants who rushed there and murdered him in the presence of doctors and left the place.

When I heard the news, I alerted Royapuram A.C. Mr. Nelson, Inspectors Kader Mohideen, Rajan and Balu, asked all vehicles to be checked and reached Royapuram police station. Luckily two rowdies involved in the murder who were attempting to escape in a lorry had been caught and were brought

The Arrested Accused in the murder case of Stanley Hospital. Vellai Ravi is fourth from the left.

to the police station. On enquiry it was learnt that others were escaping towards Tiruvotriyur . Accordingly I sent a party there. As immediate action had been taken, it was found out that Ravi and 12 others of his group were hiding in a hut in Tiruvotriyur; they were all arrested. The rowdies group did not anticipate this. If higher authorities rush to the spot, it would help solve many problems earlier.

41

The Chief Minister and a Humanitarian Approach

In Tandiarpet, Chennai there is a famous hospital for treating infectious diseases. There are plenty of trees in the compound and many old buildings. We had some information that taking advantage of some of the secluded, dark areas in the compound, some anti-social elements were stacking brought illicit liquor from Andhra Pradesh.

Ramar and two more constables from Royapuram Police station were asked to keep a watch in that area and gather information. They were in mufti on the night of December 7, 1991 and were monitoring the area. They saw a van parked there under suspicious circumstances. When they went near the vehicle, the driver suddenly started driving the van. Ramar lunged forward, had a grip on the door where the driver was seated and tried to prevent the van speeding away. But the driver not only did not stop the vehicle but in full speed proceeded and also made Ramar dash against the walls of the buildings. In spite of severe wounds, Ramar did not loosen the grip on the door of the van. The other constables had the presence of mind to rush towards the main entrance and closed the door. For sometime the van was moving within the compound and Ramar too precariously hanging on. Finally near the main entrance

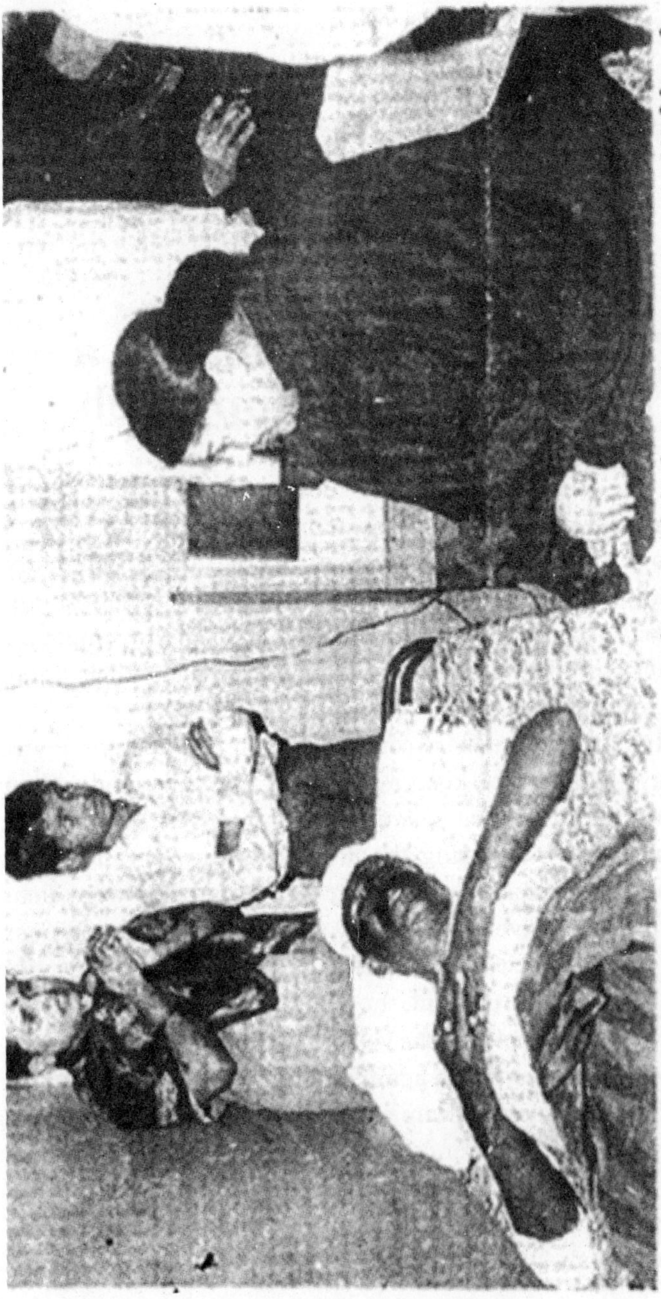

Chief Minister J. Jayalalitha consoling and complenenting Ramar, a Police constable at Stanley Hospital Chennai.

driver Chandrababu and one Ravi were arrested and 20 bags containing illicit liquor satchels were confiscated.

I went to Royapuram police station immediately, appreciated Ramar and two other constables and arranged to admit the injured constables at Stanley Hospital.

On December 8th I acquainted Mr.Rajagopalan, Commissioner and I.G. Mr. Alexander of Prohibition Wing with this news. They conveyed the same to Chief Minister Jayalalitha. Quite unexpectedly the Chief Minister visited the Hospital early in the morning and consoled the injured constables. Not only that, Ramar who had very bravely tackled the situation as in the movies had a special word of appreciation from the Chief Minister who said, "Please accept a small token of our appreciation for your heroic deed." And awarded a cash presentation of Rs.10, 000.

Ramar had retired from service. One day early in the morning when I was going for a walk, I saw him near Armenian Street, Parry's Corner. I was happy to see him with the same physique as he was in service. He also recalled with gratitude and the humanitarian concern of the Chief Minister.

42

Vinayakar Procession in Chennai – Challenge to Inter-Religious Rarmony

After the demolition of Babri Masjid on December 6, 1992 the Vinayakar Procession in Chennai every year had become a challenge to inter-religious harmony. From the day of Vinayaka Chaturthi till the following Sunday in many areas big idols would be kept for pooja and worshipped; thereafter idols from different areas would be brought to Tiruvallikeni Tiruvetteswaran temple. All the idols then would be taken in a procession and Hindu organisations and RSS after Yama gantam, exactly after 1.30 p.m. and via ice house mosque, big street reach Marina and the idols would be immersed. From Tiruvallikeni Tiruvatteswaran temple to Ice house mosque, the distance is hardly one kilo metre. But the procession would take about 3 hours to cross the same. The reason was there would be evening prayers in the mosque and it will start at 4.00 p.m. Even Imam would lead the prayer silently. The people in the procession would beat their drums and blow other instruments making great noise and this would lead to tension between who prayed in the mosque and the processionists. Sometimes it wood lead to near clashes.

Competent police officials and general public who were keen on averting clashes would ensure everything goes off smoothly.

In 1991, when Vinayaka Chaturthi was round the corner, Commissioner Mr. R. Rajagopalan called both the parties to ensure peaceful conduct of the procession. As Deputy Commissioner I along with other D.C.s Mr.Ramarajan, Radhakrishna Raja, Intelligence Superintendent participated in the meeting.

Organisers of the procession were told to start it by 1.30 afternoons and cross the Ice House mosque before 3.30 p.m. They were told to stop beating the drum etc. when they cross mosque. They should not throw colour powders on the public. They were to give assurances to abide by these. It was told to people in charge of the mosque that after midday prayer nobody should go there. Also there should be no crowding around the area. Evening prayers also must be peaceful.

Security arrangements from Tiruvallikeni Tiruvetteswaran temple were entrusted to Central region Police Commissioner Mr. Ramanujam and South region Deputy Commissioner Mr. Radhakrishna Raja. In the Ice House Mosque area I was put in charge of security arrangements. The procession started exactly at 1.O.clock. But it stopped at the junction of Tiruvallikeni High Road and Pycrofts road corner. Despite urgings from police it did not move at all. Exactly at 3.45 p.m. when in the mosque 'azar' prayer call started the procesion came near it with great noise from drums and all. Young Muslims were agitated over it and raised slogans. At one stage the organisers of the procession conducted many dance items and beating of drums opposite the mosque, threw colour powder over the public. Chappals were also thrown inside the mosque. Commissioner Rajagopalan requested the processionists to proceed with the procession but it did not have much effect. Even his cap fell in the ground and colour powders were thrown at him also. After all these, only by 6.30 pm. the procession crossed the mosque. Thereafter the procession

Indian Expr[ess]

MADRAS MONDAY SEPTEMBER 19 1994

[V]inayaka chaturthi procession peaceful

[illegible]

reached Marina, all the idols were immersed. We took care to see that nothing untoward happened when everybody returned back.

This went on till 1996. During 1991-1994, when I was the Deputy Commissioner I was in charge of security arrangements. Thereafter when I became S.P. Narcotics Intelligence Bureau, Mr. Vaikunth was DGP and Mr.V.K. Rajagopalan was the Commissioner. I took up security arrangements for the procession. D.G.P. Vaikunth wrote in Tughlaq Weekly Dated 20.12.2000 issue praising my services. My services were also appreciated in the front page of The Indian Express on September 14, 1994. Mr. Vaikunth had stated: "I was very much shocked to see the activities of anti-social elements under the garb of Vishwa Hindu Parishad during Vinayaka idols procession. Particularly while crossing the mosque, they deliberately shouted unedifying comments against Muslim religion which hurt people of Muslim community; it could have provoked retaliation. But I intervened and managed to ably save the situation. Also efficient police officers were there like Deputy Commissioner Mohamed Ali." This was a testimony to my services.

Mr.Viswanathan of VHP retorted to the comments of Mr.Vaikunth on Bandobust arrangements by expressing controversial ideas in Tughlaq issue of 3.1.2001. "Can Mr.Vaikunth make Mr.Mohamed Ali arrange for welcoming Vinayaka idol procession in front of the mosque?" Mr.Vaikunth retorted, "That is not my job. It could well be asked whether Hindus would inaugurate Muharam procession."

43

The Rescue of Kidnapping Victim Led to the Arrest of Currency Doubling Gang

While I was Dy. Commissioner of Police, Law and Order, Chennai, in 1993 there was an incident of kidnapping of a business man, and how we were able to rescue him and unravel a currency doubling racket.

Jinna was an owner of a leather factory at Perambur. His wife reported to Otteri Police Station on 15.6.1993 stating that her husband who left his residence in his jeep to leather factory was abducted midway leaving his driver by one Uniformed Inspector and 3 others who came in a car. The 'Police Inspector' took him to Maraimalainagar, which is 30 KM away from Chennai. The gang leader, Rafiq, a known criminal from Tirunelveli, locked him in a house and tortured him demanding Rs.10 lakhs. Unbearable by torture Jinna phoned up his wife, Banu, to part with the money. The intelligent Banu, accompanied with the family friend, Mastan, rightly informed the police on time.

On information I swung into action by forming the special party under ACP Mr. Ramamoorthy and Inspector Mr. Muthuvel. The party analysed the list of kidnappers and recent release of jail birds. Among them the name of Rafiq came prominent since both Jinnah and Rafiq hailed from Tirunelveli Dist. Immediately the associates of Rafiq lodged in Chennai Central Prison were contacted to find out the possible hideout of Jinnah.

Extensive searches were conducted in Guindy industrial estated, Alandur and Tambaram. At last the location of Rafiq was found out in Maraimalainagar. The police team stormed the house at night and nabbed the so called Inspector of Police and 3 others. Jinnah was untied and rescued. He was in a state of shock. Later of Rafiq was also nabbed. Among the arrested were, Balasubramaniam acted as a Police Inspector and Baskaran, a dismissed policeman.

When enquired Balasubramaniam told that the gang was also Indulging in the doubling currencies. The gang's modus operandi was that they used to buse the prospective businessmen with the promise of giving the doubling of currencies by showing a suite case containing the wire connecting with the simple machineries and batteries. Balasubramaniam will act as Inspector by descending on the scene when the transaction takes place.

The swift action by the police alone will result in rescuing the victims from the kidnappers on time, the harassment of the family members and mental agony.

44

Police Parade - Parade Commander

It is the practice in the Police Department to have Ceremonial Parade on Republic Day, Indpendence Day and when police personnel are awarded medals. After completing training for Dy. S.P. Post at Police Training College in Vellore in 1976, I was posted for training in Madurai under City S.P. Mr. Rajasekaran Nair. He asked me to command the parade on the Republic Day parade that year itself. Mr. Natarajan was the District Collector then. On 26.1.1976 the parade was held at Madurai Armed Reserve Force grounds. Every body appreciated me for commanding the parade within a few days after my joining the post.

Thereafter, I took charge as Dy.S.P. Law & Order, Coimbatore City on February 2, 1977. Mr. Panchapakesan was S.P. then and Mr. Narasimhan, the District Collector. I conducted the Independence Day Parade that year in V.O.C.Grounds and earned appreciation from everyone.

After 15 years, when I was working as Superintendent, Forest Cell CID, Presidential medal award ceremony was held at Chennai Rajarathinam Police Stadium on 26.12.1992. Even though I was in Forest Cell CID, Mr. Sripal, the then DGP and the police commissioner Mr. Rajagopalan asked me, 46 yeas old

at that time, to conduct the special parade even though there were a number of young officers. I and my Deputy Commander Reserve Force ADSP Mr. Balaram Naidu gave training with great care to the constables and conducted the parade in the presence of the Governor, Mr. Bhishma Narayan Singh. The DGP, Mr.Sripal wrote a letter commending my efficiency during January 1993. At that time I felt that I too should get President's medal through Governor. I got the prestigious President's medal for meritorious service in 2000.

45

Anti-Social Elements' Threat to Fair Price Shops Put an End to

Mr.V. Pandian, Joint Registrar of Cooperative Services wrote a letter to me on 3.9.1991 stating that in fair price shops run by the cooperative unions in North Chennai there is a threat by anti-social elements demanding 'mamools' and that these elements indulge in smuggling out essential commodities from the shops. Immediately I swung into action.

I posted near each fair-price shop in North Chennai a constable in mufti, have a check while essential commodities were distributed, monitor the employees when they close the shops and lock the doors in the night and find out who were the people threatening the employees. A confidential report was prepared and arrangements were made to capture them. During these activities, once in Tondiarpet 342 fair price shop, we stopped a van which was full of rice taken from it. We also arrested the ration shop assistant who was also a party to it. As a result of these intense activities under my direction, malpractices in fair-price shops were controlled. On 31.12.1991 Mr.V. Pandian, I.A.S., Joint Registrar of Cooperative Societies wrote a letter of appreciation: "By your immediate action, you have completely stopped the activities of anti-social elements in the above fair-price shop. I am expressing my gratitude for the same." But nobody can deny that the ration shops rice intended to be distributed for the poor people are being smuggled out from the ware house corporation itself, taken to rice mills, polished and then come to whole sale shops for sales in exorbitant prices. This is not possible without the connivance of officials from bottom to top and also political bigwigs.

46

Muslim League Factions Unite – a New Conference

Indian Muslim League was functioning under the leadership of Mr.Abdul Samad and National League under Abdul Latif at Tamilnadu. Due to these factions, Muslims were not able to get adequate representation in the state legislature or Parliament.

After negotiations between these two Muslim league parties, it was decided to integrate both the factions, and a new uprising Conference would be held in Chennai and also a grand procession. In 1992 some anti-social elements had infiltrated into Milad festivities to mark the birth day of Prophet Mohamed and had murdered three Muslims. In fact police resorted to firing to put down those indulged in violence.

So it was decided to organise on February 20, 1993 Muslim League integration procession and meeting in the evening at Marina beach. Commissioner of Police, Mr.R. Rajagopalan entrusted me with the responsibility of smooth conduct of both events. I also consulted with the organisers and arranged for suitable protection throughout the procession route. It started from Teynampet Kamaraj grounds and proceeded via Anna Salai and Royappettai. There was big turn out in the meeting place as well. Arrangements were made so that nothing untoward happened and people participated in both the events with great peace of mind.

Appreciating the smooth conduct, Mr.A.K. Abdul Samad, President of Muslim League wrote a letter to me on 22.2.1993 in which he stated: "The way you provided security and co-operation, and the manner in which officers and men discharged their duties under your leadership and for you too particularly, deserve to be commended. On behalf of our community we express our gratitude." Similarly Janab Kaja Mohideen of Muslim League also wrote a letter on 22.2.1993 expressing his gratitude.

47

Police Stalls in Government Exhibitions are Good Educational Grounds for Boosting Police Image

During 1981-82 I was working as Dy. S.P. at Tallakulam, Madurai. In Madurai Government arranges Exhibitions during Chitrai festival times. The S.P. Madurai entrusted me with the responsibility of seeing that Police Stall is made attractive and informative. The District Collector at that time was Mr.Avudaia Pillai and the Director of Exhibitions was former District Collector, Mr.K.A. Sundaram. Our stall was adjudged the best stall. As it was the first time the department had taken pains to attract people who come to festival and exhibition to lure to the police stall. We explained many technological facets in a very admirable way. On the concluding day of the exhibition, a Committee under the Chairmanship of Mr.Tamizhkudimagan, Principal Yadva College (subsequently Speaker, Tamil Nadu Legislative Assembly) had been formed and it chose our stall as the best one. Mr.K.A. Sundaram, I.A.S., Director of Exhibitions gave away the prizes to me. The District Collector Mr.Avudaiya Pillai presided over the function.

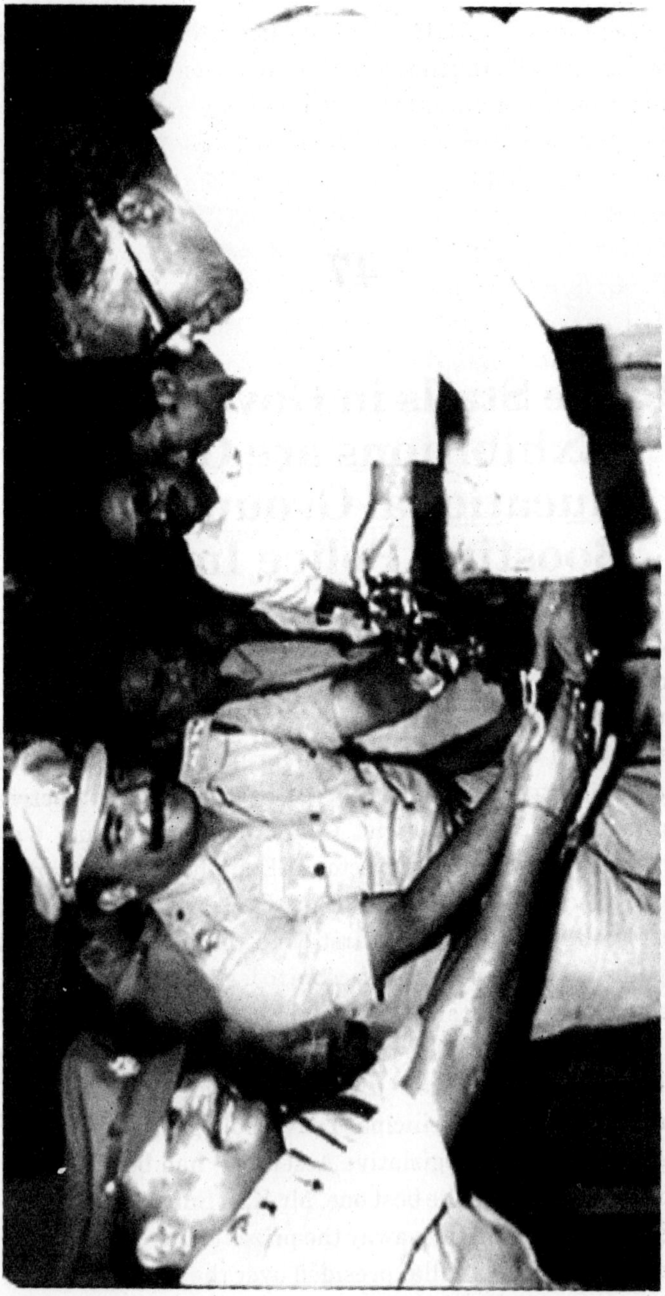

Receiving of price for police stall from Hon'ble Minister Mr. R.M. Veerappan at Salem in the year 1986.

Thereafter, in 1986 I had assumed the charge as S.P. Salem District. During the course of the year an exhibition was conducted on the grounds behind the old Salem Bus Stand. The police department also put up a stall. We had created the façade on the model of Kattabomman's fort. Not only that, we had a sound and light programme displaying the work of police department. Hearing about the niceties in our stall, former D.G.P. Mr. K. Ravindran, the I.G. Mr. Vaikunth, Vellore D.I.G. Mr. Neilwall also visited the same and appreciated sound and light programme. Mr.RM.Veerappan, Tourist Department Minister admiringly went around our stall and gave us the first prize.

In 1991, I was working as Deputy Commissioner in Chennai. At that time about Pongal time, in the Tamil month of Thai, an exhibition was held. I was entrusted with the responsibility of designing the police stall. It was on the model of Chennai Fort. To attract people we used to have Police Band in the evenings; besides our dogs squad was pressed into service which considerably generated admiration among the public. Our stall got the first prize that year. Even today our stalls in different exhibitions educate people about the activities of our department, which is a remarkable police-public relation exercise.

48

The Death of a New College Student and a Humane Act

I did my graduation course in New College, Chennai from 1966 to 1969. In 1993, when I was Dy. S.P. (Law & Order) North Chennai, I had to acquaint myself with one students' struggle in the New College.

On August 22, 1993 one Anwar Sadat belonging to Kodaikanal, who was studying in the first year at New College and also a hostelite, while travelling in a government bus fell down from the bus near the college. The injured student was taken to Royapettai Government Hospital but despite medical attention succumbed to injuries. The other hostel students who were unable to bear the shock of the loss of a friend announced that his death was due to negligence in the government hospital and began an agitation blocking traffic in Peters Road where the college was located. At that time Mr. Baskar was the Deputy Commissioner, Law and Order, in South Chennai.

D.G.P. Mr. Sripal knew that I was an old student of New College. He phoned me up and asked me to go over to New College and help Mr.Baskar to pacify the students. I also rushed there. But in the meanwhile students had damaged some buses. I and Mr. Baskar held discussions with the students. Along with us Mr. Jailani, Principal was also there. The students wanted action to be taken against the Bus driver and the doctor at Royappettai hospital who according to them did not treat the deceased Sadat properly. We told them that a case would be filed against the bus driver and students' complaint against the doctor would be forwarded to his higher authorities. But the students wanted the driver and doctor to be immediately arrested.

Then we asked the students whether anybody belonged to the same native place as the deceased. There were some students from native Kodaikanal. We asked whether his parents were informed and whether they were coming. They said that as it was night time it would be difficult to leave Kodaikanal, a hilly resort, immediately. I, Mr.Baskar and Jailani after discussion decided that if post-mortem were conducted on the body of Sadat at the night itself, the body could be sent to Kodaikanal and we could tackle the agitation of the students the following day. The doctors at Royapettai hospital conducted the post-mortem in the night itself. We told the boys that we were arranging for a vehicle to send the body to Kodiakanal. All the hostel students reached the hospital and paid respects to the deceased. Around 3.00 a.m. an ambulance carrying the body left for Kodaikanal. Students who witnessed our urgent and humanitarian action appreciated us and left peacefully for the hostel. The college also functioned smoothly the following day after brief mourning.

Anwar Sadat's father Thanga Miran and his brother Adam Malik in their letters of 24th and 23 August 199(3) respectively had appreciated my humane action in the matter.

49

Chennai Police which Helped Arrest an Andhra Spurious Liquor Dealer

When criminals escape from one state, the officials of that state usually get in touch with other state police to seek assistance to nab them. This reciprocal help is quite common.

Under such background I helped the Andhra Police to arrest some dealers of spurious liquor, who were responsible for the death of a number of people after consuming what they supplied to them. In December 1993, the Hyderabad Police were in search of one Dharmichand (27) who was dealing in spurious liquor. They had information that he was hiding in Chennai. The Police Commissioner of Hyderabad, Mr.Dinesh Reddy formed a special squad and had sent it to Chennai requesting the Chennai Police Commissioner help in this regard. The squad met with Mr. Rajagopalan bringing with them a letter asking for help. Mr. Rajagopalan called me and said that in North Chennai a lot of Marwaris were living and that I must search for the criminal with their help and arrest him.

I invited a number of prominent Marwaris and acquainted them with the tragedy of death due to spurious liquor and sought their cooperation in nabbing the criminal who is reputed to

ஆந்திராவிலிருந்து தப்பி வந்த கள்ளச் சாராய ஆசாமி சென்னையில் பிடிபட்டான்

பிடித்துக் கொடுத்ததற்காக தமிழக போலீசுக்கு நன்றி

கமிஷனர் ராஜகோபாலனுக்கு ஐதராபாத் போலீஸ் டி.ஐ.ஜி கடிதம்

have been hiding in Chennai. I told them to keep their eyes and ears wide open and pass on any useful information. They knew me well because when they had the inaugural function of big Jain temple in the Mint Street and on the opening ceremony of Jain temple in Vepery Jain's College, I had made special bandobust (security) arrangements.

The Marwaris in Sowcarpet made inquiries duly and informed me that such a person was not in that area and asked me to find out from New Washermenpet where there were some Marwari families. I had known there a dhobi (washerman) who had killed a Pawn-broker Marwari's wife as I had arrested him. Also I knew some Marwaris there. Discreet enquiries revealed that Darmichand was hiding in a house. I arrested him and handed over to the special squad.

Appreciating my services in this regard, Mr. Dinesh Reddy, Hyderabad Police Commissioner wrote a letter to Mr. Rajagopalan, Chennai Police Commissioner in which he stated, "I express my gratitude to you and Chennai City Police force in capturing Dharmichand, spurious liquor dealer who was hiding there. I particularly wish to express my gratitude to North Chennai Deputy Commissioner and the force under his supervision." (Courtesy: Makkal Kural, 16.12.1993).

50

Night Patrolling in Chennai – Arrest of Auto Drivers Who Were Robbers

On 24th of January 1994, I had night patrolling duty. Each Deputy Commissioner will be assigned a night duty. At that time Deputy Commissioner (Law & Order), 2 Crime Branch Deputy Commissioners, 1 Traffic D.C. all will form a group. The night patrol duty will start at 10.00 pm and will last till 5.00 a.m. There will be surprise inspection of police stations and checking whether fingerprints are correctly collected, whether the constables are alert, whether night patrolling is being done properly etc. It shall also be the responsibility of the Deputy Commissioner to check crimes or accidents and take immediate action.

When I was Deputy Commissioner for North Chennai, Mr.Ramarajan was the D.C. for Central Chennai and Mr.Radhakrishnaraja for South Chennai. On 24.1.1994 during night patrol Mr.Rajendra Babu, Inspector of New Washermenpet and two constables were with me.

After seeing a film at Udhayam theatre, Ashok Nagar around 11.30 p.m. Mr.Vijay Kumar, his wife Philomena, their relation Malathi, Valmikinathan their son Kadir all were

சினிமா பார்த்து விட்டு திரும்பிய

பெண்ணுக்கு கத்திக்குத்து நகை கொள்ளை

மர்ம மனிதர்கள் தப்பினார்கள்

"ஆட்டோ" டிரைவர் கைது

returning to Besant Nagar via Guindy industrial estate. They were from Kalakshetra Arundale Beach Road. An auto overtook the auto in which they were travelling and then prevented them from moving further. Three people got down from the auto, brandished knives and escaped with gold chain, bangles and ring worn by Philomena. We had finished our patrolling near Ashok Nagar and had come near Guindy industrial estate about that time. We proceeded towards where the auto had left. Near Guindy toll gate we found the auto had been proceeding. We moved fast, overtook the auto and stopped it. Auto drivers Bhaskaran and Babu were arrested. Two people had escaped from it. The jewels robbed from Philomena were safely recovered.

Mr. Sripal, DGP, would sometimes sit late in the night and listen to wireless messages and monitor what was going on in Chennai. He had followed our message to control room about robbery and how were trying to trace the robbers. He also subsequently heard the message through the wireless that we got hold of the robbers and recovered the robbed articles. He called me via wireless, congratulated and asked me to meet him in his office the following day along with Inspector and constables. On 25.1.1994 accordingly I met him along with the Inspector and constables. He very much appreciated this. Thina Thanthi and Makkal Kural had published this as news item.

51

Straight Forward Approach – Political Interference

When I was the Deputy Commissioner for North Chennai I had to confront with this politically influential person. He was a great obstacle in chasing and rounding up rowdies. At that time Boxer Vadivelu and Malaikkan Selvam had formed different groups and were constantly engaging themselves in despicable acts in the port area. One Ayodhikuppam Veeramani (later on killed in police encounter) was functioning as an enemy of Selvam. Boxer Vadivelu and Malaikkan Selvam were arrested, put in prison and subsequently let out on bail and were asked to be away from this district. This influential ruling party politician had stressed that Selvam must be permitted inside North Chennai. But I was very firm. One day he was standing outside the legislature, saw me and shouted, "I will talk to Commissioner." Ultimately he was successful. I was transferred from North Chennai and posted as SP in Narcotics Intelligence Bureau. The then DGP informed me about this personally over the telephone. This is but one incidence when we see influential leaders of the ruling party interfere in the administration and treat the officers roughly!

52

Even Truth Sometimes Becomes a Casualty

In 1993 MDMK got split from the DMK. One time gang leader Elumalai was Secretary of North Chennai MDMK. The inaugural function was a grand affair with a procession from Parry's Corner to Royapuram. Then he conducted the first conference there. After about one and a half years while he was in a cycle company, around ten in the night he was murdered. His followers indulged in violence on hearing the news. They stopped vehicles plying on the Royapuram Bridge. I, A.C. Nelson and A.C. Gunam swung into security actions. We went to Elumalai's house and assured his wife that we will definitely find out the murderers. Then we were discussing the matter and A.C. was telling that a case must be registered in Royapuram Police Station. At that time Deputy Commissioner (Crimes) came there along with some of his officers. After a little while some MDMK leaders also had come. At that time there was a telephone call to me from the Commissioner. He said, "The Crimes division would look into this. You attend to Law and Order." This sudden instruction gave me a shock.

When the case was registered, there was reference about the son of Mr. M. Karunanidhi, DMK leader, former M.L.A. of Royapuram, and some prominent leaders of Royapuram area and some others. The former DMK M.L.A. and two others were arrested. When the news that son of DMK leader was to be arrested got around there was some excitement everywhere. But when there was protest from DMK this proposal was given up. The DC of the Crimes division was transferred and Mr. O. Sundaramurthy took charge as the new D.C. Crimes division.

He had worked under me as AC. at Pulianthoppu. Both of us discussed the matter and decided that real culprits must be found out. Under Inspector Kaseef a team was formed. They conducted intense investigations. One Tikka Raman, a rowdy and some others were nabbed in June. The car used by them was confiscated; also the weapons used during the gruesome murder which had been tied in a bundle and thrown into a well were recovered. Investigations revealed that there were disputes between Raman and Elumalai over cable connection for TVs and as Raman's supporters had been driven out of Royapuram area, they murdered Elumalai as an act of vengeance.

I explained all these details first to Mr. Rajagopalan, the Commissioner. He understood the background and said that the following day all of us would meet higher officials. Accordingly, the Commissioner, Mr. Sundaramurthy, D.C. Crimes and I met with higher officials and informed them about the real culprits and details of investigation. We wanted the three leaders of DMK who were innocent to be released and charge sheet filed against the real criminals. But they said, "Who should bell the cat? You will face problems if you open this topic." We returned very much disappointed. But as we persisted with the matter real culprits were arrested and produced in the Court.

When they learnt that real culprits had been arrested, the former M.L.A. of DMK and two others produced a petition in the Court praying for their release. They wee released. This is just to indicate that sometimes even if truth comes to light the department is helpless due to certain extraneous considerations.

53

Drive on Smuggling of Narcotics

Argentinean Madonna, who was regarded as one of the greatest football players of the 20th century became an addict to narcotic substance and lost his earnings to the tune of several millions of dollars, his health and fame due to that. In an interview given in 1996 he said, "A man who becomes an addict to narcotic, has to fight against the drug each day."

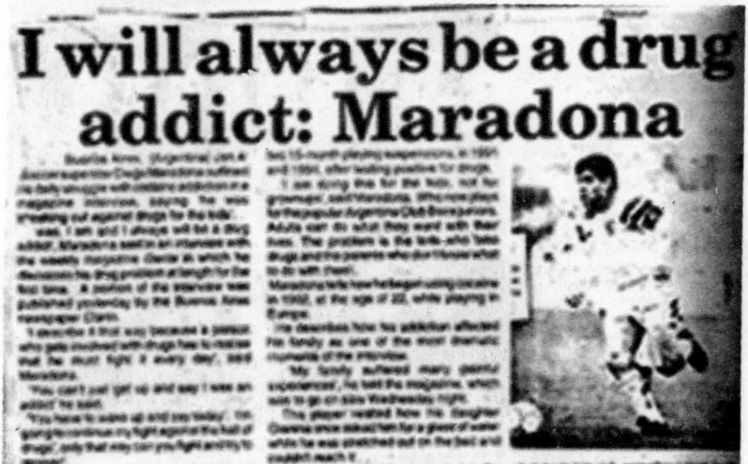

I will always be a drug addict: Maradona

He then added: "One day as I was in the height of intoxication due to drug addiction, my young daughter asked me to get a cup of water for her. I was lying in bed and she prodded me and asked for water. But even though I wanted to get up, I could not do so: I felt as if I was nailed to the bed. This was the result of my consuming cocaine. My daughter asked me, 'Can't you even give me a cup of water?' Those words haunted me throughout later on."

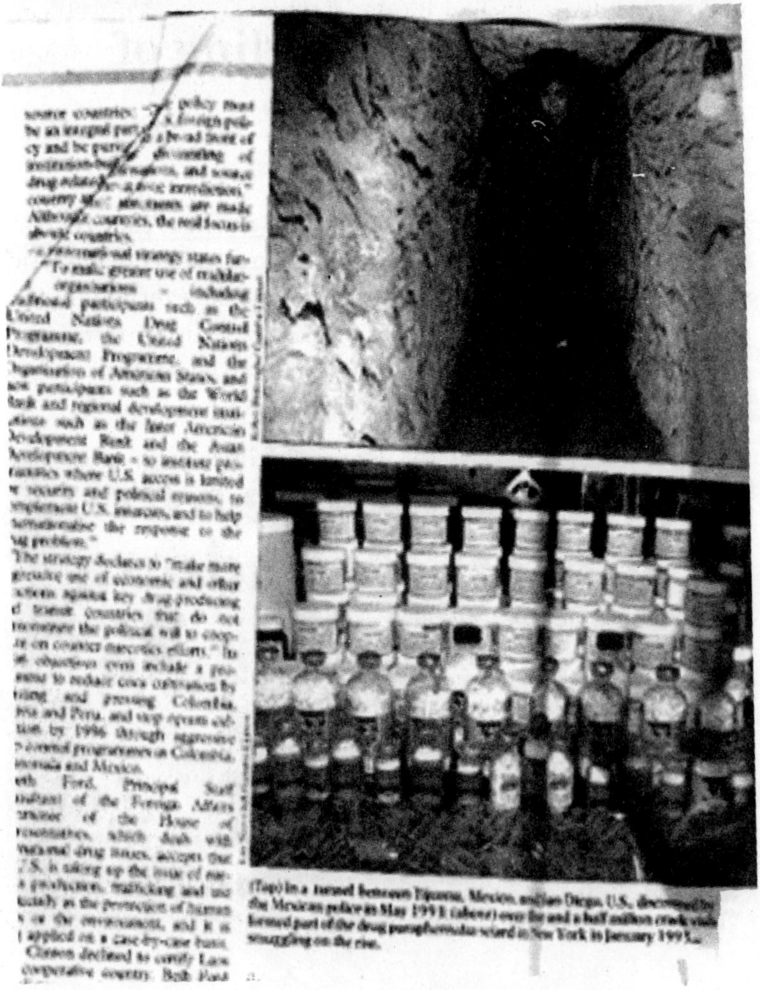

I was serving for nearly one and half years in Narcotics Intelligence Bureau during 1994-95. Agriculturalists and casual labourers consume toddy generally extracted from coconut and Palmyra trees, country liquor, a drink extracted from kasakasa, called Bosca by kalasis to drown their tiredness. Fishermen consume "Sundi Choru" a rice mixture buried under sand for a few days and then taken out and fomented with some mixtures. Students and youngsters consume narcotics like cocaine, heroin, opium, ganja, hashish, Charas, mentrax, pethedin, tidijegic injection and catamine. In the recent times boys who pick up rags smoke emanating from a paste which is used to fill in the puncture of tyres.

சென்னை ஓட்டலில்

ரூ.1½கோடி போதை மருந்து பறிமுதல்

3 பேர் கைது

Cocaine is a narcotic prepared from a plant called cocaine. This is manufactured in South America and used by Americans. Heroin powder is gathered from poppy seeds (kasakasa). These are primarily cultivated in what is referred to as the golden triangle, i.e., junction of Afghanistan, Pakistan and North West frontier areas of India. (Also in Utter Pradesh and Madhya Pradesh states). As we gather rubber from a milk-like substance after scratching rubber plant, so also when poppy seeds are scratched, a blackish paste like substance emerges which is dried up and refined. This is opium. A very minute particle of this has the property to cure stomach disorders. Only the District Collectors in India are given the powers to permit such extraction for medicinal purposes. This opium is chemically treated with ascetic anhydride coming out as waste from sugar-cane crushing factories and then heroin powder is refined. From that one gets charas. Near the border areas there are regular (illegal) factories for manufacture of heroines. We recently witnessed an Engineer in Rajasthan using his garage itself to manufacture heroin! Of course, he was arrested.

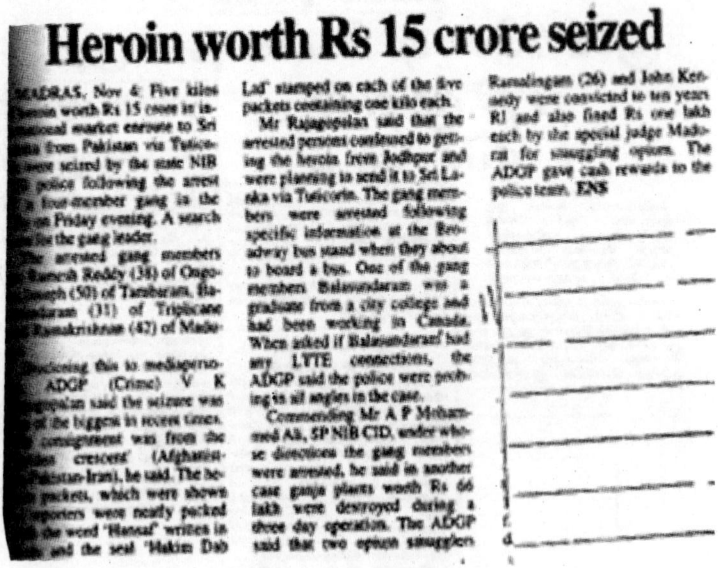

Heroin worth Rs 15 crore seized

MADRAS, Nov 4: Five kilos heroin worth Rs 15 crore in international market enroute to Sri Lanka from Pakistan via Tuticorin were seized by the state NIB police following the arrest of a four-member gang in the city on Friday evening. A search is on for the gang leader.

The arrested gang members are Ramesh Reddy (38) of Ongole, Joseph (50) of Tambaram, Balasundaram (31) of Triplicane and Ramakrishnan (42) of Madurai.

Disclosing this to mediapersons, ADGP (Crime) V K Rajagopalan said the seizure was one of the biggest in recent times. The consignment was from the golden crescent (Afghanistan-Pakistan-Iran), he said. The heroin packets, which were shown to reporters were neatly packed with the word 'Hansaf' written in ... and the seal 'Hakim Dab Lal' stamped on each of the five packets containing one kilo each.

Mr Rajagopalan said that the arrested persons confessed to getting the heroin from Jodhpur and were planning to send it to Sri Lanka via Tuticorin. The gang members were arrested following specific information at the Broadway bus stand when they about to board a bus. One of the gang members Balasundaram was a graduate from a city college and had been working in Canada. When asked if Balasundaram had any LTTE connections, the ADGP said the police were probing in all angles in the case.

Commending Mr A P Mohammed Ali, SP NIB CID, under whose directions the gang members were arrested, he said in another case ganja plants worth Rs 66 lakh were destroyed during a three day operation. The ADGP said that two opium smugglers Ramalingam (26) and John Kennedy were convicted to ten years RI and also fined Rs one lakh each by the special judge Madurai for smuggling opium. The ADGP gave cash rewards to the police team. ENS

Products like heroin and charas prepared in the golden triangle area are smuggled to coastal places like Tuticorin and Rameswaram through various means and sent to Sri Lanka. But if you ask the question whether Sri Lanka people are such addicts to these, the answer is 'no'. Taking advantage of internal strife, militants send these narcotics through ships anchored off Sri Lankan coastal area to Europe and far-off places. The huge profits obtained by smuggling these into Europe and selling there at fabulous price enable them to buy sophisticated armaments for their militant outfits. That helps them to kill each other and also conduct war with government.

Four kg of heroin seized

From Our Staff Reporter

MADRAS, Dec. 26.

Four kilograms of heroin, valued at Rs.4 crores in the international market, was seized by the State Narcotics Intelligence Bureau (NIB) CID police personnel following the arrest of two Sri Lankan nationals in the city today.

The Director General of Police (Crime), Mr. K. K. Rajasekharan Nair, said that acting on a tip-off and following strict vigil over such clandestine movements, a team of NIB-CID personnel picked up the two Sri Lankan nationals near the military polo ground at St. Thomas Mount. The Sri Lankans were arrested with two bags in which they were found to carry four kilograms of brown sugar concealed in "sweet packets".

The names of the two arrested were given as Shiva (29) alias Baleswaran of [illegible] who is the son of a Sri Lankan Administrative Service officer, and the other his 25-year-old friend, [illegible], a resident of Rameswaram and a native of Trincomalee.

Interrogation of the two revealed that the heroin was procured at Indore and it was meant to be smuggled out to Sri Lanka from Madras. Cases have been registered against them.

"We have already started a detailed investigation of how the two Sri Lankans were in possession of four kilogram of heroin and we are in the process of informing the Central Narcotics Control Bureau to check their national and international connections by seeking the assistance of the Interpol", said Mr. Nair.

The DGP commended the Deputy Inspector of Police, Mrs. Latika Saran, and the Superintendent of Police, Mr. A. P. Mohamed Ali, for effecting the seizure.

Mr. Nair also presented cash rewards as an incentive to the team of police officers involved in effecting the seizure. Mr. K. Pandiaraj, Inspector was given Rs. 1,000, two Sub-Inspectors — Mr. S. [illegible] and Mr. K. [illegible] received Rs. 500 each, and four Head Constables — Mr. Parthiban, Mr. Selvaraj, Mr. Jayaraj and Mr. [illegible] were presented with Rs. 250 each.

There are outfits which buy a kg of heroin, cocaine etc. for Rs.10, 000 and sell the same in American and European markets for Re.1 crore. In March 2007, in Mexico, a South American country, Police raided a residential quarters and confiscated Rs. 950 crores worth currencies of different nations, sales amount of narcotic substance! The group which had indulged in this had security measures including bunkers. In Columbia there are outfits having their own men, weapons and helicopters for protection to export the narcotics prepared from their own agricultural lands! Their arsenal has modern weapons capable of withstanding and giving counter-attacks to the army of the country! It is noteworthy here to mention they use even submarine to smuggle their contrabands.

Mantrax and Catamine are the tablet and powder forms of narcotics which are given chemical treatment. Africans largely consume them. In the recent years its use is spreading in Asian countries as well because they are not as costly as cocaine or heroin. Those who take (Tidijegic) do so by injecting the same into their bodies: their secret code word is 'inject'. The danger in this is the same needle used by many. In poor areas, lanes and by lanes, bus stands and train platforms this practice is widely prevalent. Smugglers cleverly use womenfolk to attract business for this. People collect syringes and needles thrown out from hospitals and use them to 'inject' the substance to youngsters. This leads to very rapid spread of fast killing diseases like HIV etc. I do not want to elaborate on ganja addiction as it is very widely prevalent.

After taking charge, I paid a courtesy call on Mr. P.V. Rajaraman, Home Secretary. He said, "Youngsters and students are very much affected by these narcotics. The proverb says that a crane will patiently wait till a big fish comes along. (Similarly catch hold of the big smugglers!). So recommend the big ones to be booked under the Goonda Act."

I acted accordingly and in the year 1994, 12 smugglers were put behind the bars under the Goonda Act. Under the Prevention of Narcotics Act 15 persons were convicted for 10 years and fined one lakh rupees.

Information was received about smuggling into Tamil Nadu injection needles from Andhra via Central Station in August1994 while laying in wait at the station, (1) Shahul Hamid of Ennore, (2) S.Kannan of Adambakkam, and

6 ★★★

சென்னையில், 10 மாதங்களில்

ரூ. 42 கோடி போதை மருந்த

பறிமுதல்

20 பேர் கைது

(3) Ramachandran were intercepted and it was found out that 1,150 injections were hidden under the clothes of their suit case. They had planned to sell these in the lanes and by lanes of Waltax Road and Peria Medu. They were duly arrested. (Thina Thanti 27.8.1994).

We shall now see some larger seizures. In November 1994, Mohammad Asad, Kalal, Yogaraj and Lazarus who were attempting to smuggle heroin powder and were staying at a lodge in Mannadi were arrested. Not only the narcotic substance but a gun, three bullets and knives kept by them for self-protection were also confiscated. All of them were put behind the bars. (Dinamalar 29.11.1994)

The smuggling of narcotic substance from Chennai to Sri Lanka also took place through some novel methods. In December 1994 we raided a residence at Tiruvallikeni at midnight, arrested Sibri alias Sirajuddin, Kasim and Ravichandran all from Sri Lanka who were all preparing packets of small dosages. The narcotic substances in the form of tablets will be encapsulated in very small vials. They will be swallowed by smugglers. They will be in the stomach for four hours. Beyond that period it will burst and damage the interior. Therefore these people will swallow the same before boarding on the plane and when once reach Sri Lanka immediately retrieve them through rectum. Thereafter these are smuggled into European countries. People who swallow and smuggle these vials are called 'sparrows' and get about Rs.1, 000 or Rs.2, 000. But they undertake great risks for this amount. Recently we learnt that not only such substances but even foreign and local currencies are smuggled out of a place in this fashion. (Thina Thanthi 10.12.1994)

During December, 1994, from Indore in Madhya Pradesh two young men belonging to Sri Lanka smuggling group were arrested near Pallavaram, Chennai. One of them was Siva alias Baleswaran (son of a high official in Velvettithurai): the other one was Ilanchezhian. Four kg of heroin were recovered form them. They had hidden this into a card board box of a famous sweet stall to avoid suspicion. (Thina Thanthi 27.12.1994)

In March 1995 it was found that in Vadapalani that one Gopinath was the brain behind narcotic smuggling using some cine actresses; he and one Anita were arrested in this connection. They were having one and half kg of heroin. (Makkal Kural 29.3.1995)

54

Some Prominent People Arrested for Involvement in Narcotic Smuggling

We had information that opium was being sold in Egmore, T'Nagar, Nungambakkam and Vadapalani. We monitored the activities and Sebastian of Virugambakkam, an MDMK public speaker, Pandian, Soundra Kumar of Rajasthan, Mohan owner of a lathe workshop in Tiruvotriyur and Umamaheswaran of Waltax Road were arrested. They were in possession of half a kg of opium. (Indian Express news service, June 17, 1995).

In 1995 July, on an information that heroin was being smuggled out from Tuticorin intense monitoring resulted in the arrest of one Selvaraj belonging to Ayatthurai, Srivaikuntam. About one and half kg. heroin which was to have been sent to Mumbai was recovered.

In 1995 during May, in a series of arrests for smuggling hashish five people including two drivers of government buses wee arrested. This hashish consumption is spreading fast among students and youngsters. There was a complaint that this was spreading very fast in Madurai. Accordingly investigations were made which led to the arrest of one Kallan, a driver of Madurai PRC and Muniyandi, a tea shop owner in Tirumangalam were rounded up; they were in possession of one and half kg of hashish. On the basis of information given by them one Jeevanandam of Rani Mangammaal Govt. Transport was also arrested and two kilos of hashish recovered from him. Based on information from him Sundaram of K.T.C. govt. bus transport was arrested and two kilos of hashish confiscated. One Murugan of Tuticorin was also arrested during this series of arrests. The Inspector of Madurai area Prohibition wing, Mr.Pattabhi conducted these operations with great efficiency. Mr.Rajasekaran, the then D.G.P (Crimes) greatly appreciated these. (Indian Express, May 30, 1995, Thina Thanthi 31.5.1991).

55

A Prodigy Who Lost the Chance of Becoming I.A.S. due to Bad Company

In 1995 November, Ramesh Reddy, Joseph, a conductor in K.T.C., Balasundaram, a young graduate who was working in Canada, Ramakrishna of Madurai were all arrested and a 5 kg package of heroin was recovered. (Thina Thanthi 5.11.1995)

A Customs Inspector's son was preparing for I.A.S./I.P.S examinations. The Inspector was living in Besant Nagar. The son was very intelligent but was not successful in the first attempt. He was in Canada for a while and then returned to Chennai. During that time he had contacts with Sri Lanka youth, got into the habit of heroin addiction and also began to indulge in smuggling. His father had provided him with an A.C.Room in the upstairs with all facilities. However, he rarely went up and saw how his son was getting along there. Therefore, when we arrested his son for smuggling activities and searching the room, he was terribly shocked to see needles and heroine powder and other substances. Parents should not just allot a room to the children and remain indifferent later on. They should have a watch over what is going on there. Otherwise they may go astray, like what happened to that unfortunate son.

ரூ.15 லட்சம் போதைப்பொருள் கடத்தல் இலங்கை ஆசாமி உட்பட கைது 3

Similarly whenever the narcotic in the substance form is confiscated, one should not come out with public announcement about the nature of the substance. Only after laboratory tests confirm the nature of the substance, the matter should be made public. There are people who just sell chloride powder passing it on as narcotic. Many buyers have been fooled into buying such phoney powders. Just for the sake of gaining publicity one should not rush to the press prematurely. I know the instances of people in the rank of even DGP who were in a hurry to call the press and got red faced thereafter when it turned out that it was not heroine.

56

Hunt for Ganja (charas) Cultivation and Precautions

For rearing ganja plants, forest lands in Western Ghats are chosen. In these reserved forest areas, some trees are felled, and then ganja plants are grown. These are watered with the help of rubber hoses connected to some natural fountains in the area. It will take three to four months for the plants to become full grown. To protect these plants from wild animals and also from the forest officials the garden area is fenced and small country bombs are also placed so that when any one touches the fence they go off very loudly and the owner is alerted to take appropriate steps. So these people generally will be armed with country bombs, knives, guns etc. Sometimes they dwell in thatched huts constructed right in the middle of plant garden. They will attack the police and forest officials with these weapons. Also they will mix pesticides in the food articles they had prepared so that if the raid party eats those foods the latter would be attacked with deadly diseases.

In places like Bodimettu and Chinnamanur at the top of the mountains leeches would abound in forest areas. They would place themselves in thorny bush, open their mouths widely and wait for goats, cattle or men to pass by so that they would attack

The Author along with his narcotics team in the midst of Ganja plants at Varusai nadu hill.

the fleshy part, spread their saliva and then with their teeth could suck blood. Only when their stomachs are filled with blood, would they release their hold on the flesh. The place bitten by leeches would be lightly bleeding. Those who climb mountains usually will have as precaution kerosene, shikakai powder etc. The bottom end of the trousers (pants) would be covered with socks, tied with small strings, and then the paste of shikakai powder mixed with kerosene would be spread over the cloth. That would protect from the attack of the leeches. Sometimes some constables accompanying me were a little careless in this regard and had to pay the penalty of severe attack from the leeches. Blood had oozed from their private parts, nose, ears, etc. It will take some days in fact for injury to be healed.

Varusai Nadu in Madurai District, Chinnamanur and Bodimettu in Theni district are the places where ganja plants are grown. Near Vasantha Estate in Varusai Nadu in places like Karikathykavu, Palathu Odai, Bommarajapuram etc. these plants are interspersed with Kambu and Cholam. In Theni ranges Oyyamparai, Vellampathai besides Kottakkudi reseve forest Odai in Bodimettu too these plants are constantly grown.

If many raids in Tamil Nadu results in the lower production, then Ganja would be smuggled into Tamil Nadu from Nellore and Warrangal areas of Andhra Pradesh.

When I was Superintendent of Narcotics Prevention section, the Tamil Nadu Chief Minister Jayalalitha in a speech on Police Budget dated 10.4.1995 said, "Last year our Narcotics Intelligence Bureau had created a record in their tasks. Finding that Sri Lanka Tamils were using Tamil Nadu to bring narcotic substances into their places before they are sent to western countries, our section arrested many people involved in this and confiscated huge quantities of narcotics." (Malai Malar, 10.4.1995)

57

My Services During the Communal Clashes that Shook Rajapalayam, Tirunelveli, Tuticorin and Ramanathapuram Areas

We know how we have decently treated refugees from Sri Lanka, Bangladesh and Pakistan. But Tamil Nadu which has the reputation of raising the level of those who seek refuge here saw how the caste demon raised its ugly head during 1996 and 1998 had ravaged the southern districts. When elections come we find people specialising in inciting caste and communal hatred and disrupt social harmony. In truth there are no compelling factors for the outbreak of any caste violence. But very minor wordy duels in tea-shops or in the fields, groves, shops, market streets would be converted by evil forces into violent caste clashes with free use of knifes, sickles and burning of haystacks, huts and then leading on to murder and pillage.

In the same vein, when I was functioning as Superintendent in Narcotics (Prohibition) Wing, Rajapalayam and Tuticorin were aflame with caste clashes. In Rajapalayam South Police Station was located in the market street. This is where Police officers and constables who come to the place for security work would be lodged. But the small station did not even have latrine. When once an ADGP (Crimes) wanted to ease himself. I told him to go the backside of the building. He went there, returned in a hurry and asked me whether there was any provision of urinal or lavatory. I told him that there was only open space and everyone uses only that space for easing. He was shocked, but there was no alternative, went to backyard and attended to the call of nature! Many police stations and outposts in rural areas are only like that. The police who go over there for security work would have to virtually camp out in the middle of the street. Things are now gradually improving.

In March 1992 a small verbal clash unfortunately led to violence and murder. People who were returning from cotton mills or shops or watchmen of groves, people returning after seeing a film were all indiscriminately murdered. People who were having their coconut groves near the foothills neglected to take care of them which resulted in theft of coconuts. In 1996 when the elections were announced women in Rajapalayam gathered at Bus Stand and decided not to permit the Lady Chief Minister inside the township and create a blockade.

According to them the friend of the C.M.who belonged to a particular caste only had encouraged people to attack Adi Dravidars. The task of pacifying them was given to me by ADGP Mr.Kumarasamy. I told them, "In a democracy everybody has the right to canvas for votes. You can show your protest against the visit of the C.M. by remaining in your own homes. It would not be proper to organise a road blockade." They respected my advice and the visit of the C.M. went off peacefully.

D.I.G. Mr.Dharmaraj was also in the security arrangements. Both of us used to visit places where murder had taken place and promptly arrested the suspicious ones. We also increased night patrolling. One night we received information that some who planned a communal clash had gathered in a village. As it was night time, we also took along with us the S.P. of that District. We reached the village at about midnight which was at the foot of the hills. Then the S.P. said that he was returning back as he was feeling sleepy. We both were shocked to hear such words. We told him that as he was the S.P. of the district when we arrest the violence mongers, if he were there, it would have proper approval. But if he felt sleepy, he could sleep in the car. He agreed to this suggestion and got into the car and began to sleep! We went into the village, arrested the violence-mongers and then woke up the S.P. for further action. Similar measures under ADGP (Crimes) Mr.Rajagopalan were undertaken and we arrested a gang of murderers who were hiding in a coconut grove. In that place we found evidence that they had hunted forest deer and then cooked the same. The then DGP Mr.Walter Dewaram wrote me a letter on 24.4.1996 appreciating my action in firmly putting down caste disturbances and violence in and around Rajapalayam.

In May 1996, elections to legislative assembly were held. In Tuticorin on behalf of the different parties candidates belonging to Nadar community had been contesting while the fishing community (fernando) had its own candidate. There always used to be competition between these two communities. The fishermen worked very hard to make their own candidate as the representative of the constituency.

At that time, even though I was working as Superintendent, Narcotics (Prohibition) Wing, I was entrusted with the election security arrangements in Kovilpatti, Oddappidaram and Vilathikulam areas. It is in Oddappidaram that the problematical Kodiangulam village is situated. Here Mr.Krishnasamy contested on behalf of Adi Dravidars. MDMK leader Mr.Vaiko contested from Vilathikulam. After the elections were over peacefully in the above places, I returned to Chennai. The counting of votes for Tuticorin constituency took place in V.O.C.College campus. On 9th May after the counting of votes, DMK candidate Mr.Periasamy was declared elected while Rosch of fishermen community had been defeated. Violence broke out. A group of fishermen burnt a number of houses in Pudugramam, the house of a cinema theatre and a wine shop. Also crude bombs were hurled. Violence also spread too many other places. To control it, the police resorted to firing and one fisherman was killed in that. Mr. Sekar, D.I.G. Tirunelveli, Mr. Gunaseelan, S.P. of Tuticorin, Mr. Jothi Jagarajan, District Collector were all holding the posts then. When the situation went out of control in Tuticorin, ADGP (Law&Order) Mr. Kumarasamy told me over the phone that DGP Mr. Dewaram wanted me to go to Tuticorin immediately. I said that I would leave in the morning but he insisted that I should leave in the night itself immediately. Therefore, I went by flight to Madurai. A car and a van full of striking police force waited for me there. I proceeded to Tuticorin. Around 2.00 A.M. I was nearing Tuticorin. Then in wireless we received an urgent communication. A Dy. S.P. of Prohibition Wing reported that nearly a thousand fishermen had assembled in Thracepuam with lights and weapons and that he was just there with twelve constables and requested S.P. and D.I.G. in the Control Room to send more forces there. I told him in the wireless that he need not fear and asked him to bravely stand in front of the crowd and that I would be there in five minutes. Without even visiting the D.I.G. at the office in Tuticorin, I rushed to Thracepuram with my force. When we marched towards the crowd, petrol bombs were hurled at us. Also crude country bombs were thrown at us. We were not bothered and charged at the violent crowd. When Dy. S.P. Prohibition saw this he too got courage and joined us. Mr. Abhay Kumar Singh, ASP, Tuticorin Rural, Dy. S.P. of Koilpatty Mr. Dakshinamurthy also charged advancing towards the crowd which now began to frantically disperse.

Thereafter I met M.Sekar, DIG. The following day ADGP Mr. Kumarasamy came to Tuticorin. In the meeting under his chairmanship, it was decided that firm action should be taken, not to permit people to gather in numbers and whoever indulged in violence must be severely dealt with. Accordingly all of us took steps and within three days everything was brought under control. A judicial commission was appointed to inquire into the incident. It was stated that I had taken very harsh measures to contain violence. I deposed that we had to deal very firmly with violence and we did that and that was why violence was contained and did not spread. I also said that there was the possibility of the whole extreme south coastal areas being caught up in violent clashes. My contentions were accepted. The May 31 edition of Indian Express also praised my services at that time. The Madurai Advocate, Mr.T. Jeyapal wrote a letter appreciating my work.

In Ramanathapuram district during Thevar Jayanthi, clashes between Adi Dravidars and Mukkulathors became a routine and in October since Thevar Birth day false on 30th Oct. 1998 I went to Ramanathapuram under ADGP Mr. Kumarasamy. There were many murders, robberies and many burning incidents. I.G. Mr.Manoharan did a great job in containing the same. I was asked to assist him in Ramanathapuram, Kilakkarai and R.S. Mangalam areas. All the shops were closed in R.S.Mangalam for three days. Seeing our plight, my college mate Mr.Anwar fed us. A goodwill committee with Messrs. T. Kiruttinan, Tamizhkkudimagan and Selvaraj then State Ministersas members appreciated the action taken in this area by me. I.G. Mr.Manoharan also wrote a letter appreciating my services on 23.11.1998.

58

D.G.P. Ruined by His Own Despicable Conduct!

In 1995-96, I was functioning as S.P. Narcotics (Prevention). At that time a DGP took charge as head of the Crimes division. He was due to retire from service in a few months' time. Like other officers I, too, went and paid a courtesy call to him taking files pertaining to my division. He said, "I will call you later. You may come then." I had said yes of course. After some days, he phoned me up and asked me to meet him in his office. I also took some files pertaining to my department and acquainted him with some details. Then he said that he wanted to talk with me personally and asked me to go over to his house which was in South Chennai.

I went exactly at 7 in the evening to his house. He took me to his office room which was in the upstairs of the building and gave me a cup of coffee. Then, he said, "Ali, I am due to retire in a few months' time." He then mentioned the names of some police official of his IPS Bach and said that he had become Crorepathi. And then he said, "I have not earned anything. Officials like you must help me." I asked ignorantly, "What can I do, Sir?" He said, "Well, if you are inclined, you can do this. 1) People who give information about narcotic smugglers are given some rewards from special fund. You can give me a portion from that fund every month, 2) "From Constable to Inspector persons are appointed in this department based on their good conduct only. They should be free from vices. However, a Sub-Inspector or Inspector must give me between one and a half lakhs to rupees two lakhs hereafter, 3. "I am starting a Charitable Trust in the name of my father. That is why I require large financial help."

Until then no higher authority had dared to ask bribe like this. Therefore, I was simply frozen on hearing these words. It took some time for me to recover. He said, "What, am I reasonable?" I said, "The narcotics division, NIB alone is not concerned with. NCB of Central government, Customs, and DRY are all enforcing authorities in this wing. The Tamil Nadu Narcotics division has done excellent service competing with the Central enforcing agencies. To do that due reward must be given to informers. Not only that, if we do not appoint honest people as Sub-Inspectors and Inspectors and appoint corrupt people, then the good name of the department would be spoiled." That higher official said that he was not concerned with all those things and asked me to inform him of my decision the following day. I returned to my residence in a dazed condition.

Further that DGP had taken some administrative decision which was contrary to Govt. order. M.C.B.C.I.D. set up.

Next evening the higher official telephoned me and asked me whether I had come to some decision in the matter. When I said "no", he disconnected the phone. Then I met DIG Ms. Lathika Saran, Mr. Perumalsamuy I.G. and told them about the DGP's greedy and corrupt desire. They asked me to inform ADGP Mr. V.K. Rajagopalan. I acquainted him with the details; He said he would meet DGP.

I felt that things could go beyond me. One morning I went to the Secretariat, met with the Home Secretary Thru. P.V. Raja ramân and told him about the strange demand of DGP. He said, "This is an unfortunate affair. I will look into it." I returned to my office. At 5 in the evening, I.G. Mr.Perumalsamy, DIG Lathika Saran and I were asked to go over to the Camp Office of the C.M. Jayalalitha who held an enquiry. Then she asked us to leave. Even before we returned to our homes, we heard the news that the greedy Crimes DGP had been transferred and we were relieved to learn that the department got rid of this corrupt person! But unfortunately that some corrupt police office has assumed the change of regular D.G.P. Law and Order. Within few months of taking charge his picture appreared in front page of the english national daily deserbing him as most corrupt D.G.P ever Tamil Nadu Police had seen even he was not given the eatension of service and he was allowed to realise.

59

Coastal Protection Police Force

The Border Security Force of the Central Government protects North Indian states from being infiltrated by nationals from neighbouring countries. Similarly, in Tamil Nadu to protect the coastal areas and prevent infiltration of foreign extremists and smuggling activities and to act as a goodwill bridge between the coastal people and government we have Police C.S.G. In 1991, some cadre of LTTE had infiltrated into Tamil Nadu and a suicide squad of theirs assassinated the former Indian Prime Minister Rajiv Gandhi and also killed many at Sriperumbudur. A committee under the Chairmanship of Mr. P. Rajendran, I.P.S., was formed to devise ways and means to establish a chain of centres which would protect the coastal area. On the basis of its recommendations it was decided to have 60 centres along the coast. But by 1993 only 23 centres had become operative.

After 1996 General elections since I was not well disposed of the Party in Power and that Crime DGP whom then Chief Minister transferred out became DGP of Tamilnadu. But subsequently he met the very bad name because of the corrupt practices and national English Daily reported against him in the front page unheard of about any high ranking police officer of any State. I was transferred from Narcotics (Prohibition) Wing to Coastal Security Group. I undertook inspection of areas where Check Posts or Centres had not been established. Vilundamavadi in Nagai District, Killai in Cuddalore District, Manakkudi, Sayalkudi and Pamban in Ramnad Disticts were the places where in the backdrop of the influence of smugglers, Highways and District administrations had blocked the efforts to open centres. I met Mr. Meena, Nagai District Collector, Mr.Ramanathan, Tanjore District Collector, Mr. Anand, Ramnad District Collector, Mr. Murthy, Tuticorin District Collector and got sanction for establishing centres in the areas mentioned above. Moreover, I got sanction for having Dy.S.Ps.head quarters for Tuticorn, Ramnad, Tanjore and Nagai districts. I also was able to get permission for the allotment of lands for the construction of their offices from the Revenue Commissioner for all those.

Not only was that, for the benefit of the constables and officers who are on duty provision made for construction of latrines, bath rooms and kitchens. We dug bore wells and overcame the usual water shortage in coastal area in Ramanathapuram Dt. The third check post between Dhanushkodi and Arichimunai did not have electricity. That is because in 1964 hurricane the sea water had entered Dhanushkodi town and the whole place was washed away. The Central Reserve Police and Tamil Nadu Police who were stationed there did not even have buildings and were having just temporary thatched roofs. During night times they had to manage with torch lights only. To remove these hardships I made representations to the District Collector Mr. Anand and permission was sanctioned for construction of building and a generator for producing electricity.

The Tamil Nadu Governor Ms.Fathima Beevi expressed a desire to see Arichimunai, the island separated from Rameswaram and tip of Mannar Gulf. There is a beautiful landscape and clean sea sand which are beautiful sight seeing spots from the tourist point of view. To travel smoothly on the

Inauguration of Coastal Watch Tower at Kodiakarai in 1998.

sea sands, the coastal force had given a patrol jeep in which the Governor was taken around. We also followed. We explained about the ravages due to 1964 hurricane and how the whole township had been destroyed. The remnants of railway station and some buildings could be seen. The scenic beauty of Arichimunai could be seen in a Tamil movie called "Kannathil muthamittal". The Governor was very much impressed with the beauty of the place and suggested that a memorial could be raised in honour of Dhanushkodi. I told then Ramnad M.L.A. Mr. Rehman Khan who was also a minister about this. He took up this matter and now a memorial stands in the place. Also for monitoring sea tigers, extremist group, a watch tower was constructed in Kodiakkarai. At the base of the watch tower rooms were constructed for stay of police officers. Mr. Alexander, I.P.S. had opened these facilities. Similarly without spoiling the aesthetic beauty of Marina beach, near the old DGP office, a new building was constructed for the Coastal Guard Police. For the first time in the police buildings a lift was provided there. I had taken much care in the construction of check posts, regional office buildings for Dy. S.P.s and the Headquarters building. I also recommended to Mr.Alexander that the Headquarters building be named as "Neidal Illam", meant the building intended for the sea and its surroundings. But when the building was declared open for use, both of us were in different wings. Mr. Alexander has mentioned my service in an article in a book on History of Tamil Nadu Police Force.

60

Check-Posts to Contain Many Smuggling Activities

In Ramnad District, Sri Lanka militants indulged in armed robbery in a village called Valasai and our prompt action enabled arrest of those involved.

On 31.8.1998 in a village called Nadar Valasai under the jurisdiction of Alagankovil Police Station, Ramnad District, two persons with machine guns had entered a wine ship, threatened people there, beat them up, fired a round or two towards the sky and decamped with looted money. ADGP Mr. Alexander directed then I.G. Mr.V.Balachander and myself to proceed by car immediately to Ramnad and said we should not return to Chennai without capturing them. We left immediately and reached Ramanathapuram in the morning. We had a meeting with Mr. Sakthivelu, S.P. and others. We came to the conclusion that they could be hiding in the bush in marshy area and decided to search every square inch in the area. Also arranged to strengthen the police force in each check post and also gave them modern pistols and automatic guns. Day and night we visited such places like Nadar Valasai, Therinpothu Sembaiarkulam, Ammari, Devipattinam, Panaikkulam,

Gopiarmadam, Athankaai, Muniverappattinam, Sittarkottai and Alagankulam villages and searched for the criminals.

During that hunt, we also arrested one Irulandi a habitual robber who had robbed from a blind old man a sum of Rs. 3, 070/- in the evening of 3.9.1998. When we were searching for the criminals on 4.9.1998 near Gopiarmadam village saltpans, two militants were trying to escape from near the check-post. When these militants were attempting to retrieve two AK 47 guns which they had buried near the bush, the check post staff surrounded them with sophisticated weapons and forced them to surrender. The militants finding that they could not escape surrendered. Then we confiscated their two AK 47 machines guns, 216 bullets, and the money which had been robbed. Then we brought them to Ramnad SP's office and investigated. We learnt that both of them belonged to TELO militant outfit of Jaffna and that fearing that anytime LTTE could wipe them out had escaped to Tamil Nadu. One Mr.Mari had given him shelter and also suggested how the wine shop could be robbed. We also arrested Mari. As our actions were swift and quick as we see sometimes in pictures, we were able to arrest them, capture the guns and recover the money. Mr. Balachander, I.G. wrote to ADGP Mr. Alexandar, "Sir, Mr. Muhamed Ali, D.I.G. conducted the operation in a very swift manner which enabled us to capture three criminals."

61

Lost Gun while Asleep, Subsequently Recovered

Tirukkadaiyur in Nagai District has a temple famous for attracting people who would perform their 60th year completion worship. From the township, on the way to coast there is a Check-post. Constables used to perform their duties here. In 1998 during December I was observing Ramzan fasting. At 4 a.m. early in the morning there was a telephone call form Mr. Alexander, ADGP who asked me to meet him in house in full uniform. Accordingly I went to his house. He said, "Ali, in Tirukkadaiyur Check-post, it appears that a gun is missing. The DGP Mr. Sharma has informed me. Shall we proceed?" I told him that he need not trouble himself and that I would go over there. I told Dy. S.P. Ramasamy of the incident and both of us left for Tirukkadaiyur which we reached by 2.00 P.M.

During my inquiry we learnt that on the previous night between 12 midnight and 3 in the early morning the duty constable's .303 gun seems to have been missing. This was noticed by the constable whose duty timings were between 3.00 a.m. and 6.00 a.m. The matter was immediately communicated to the nearest police station. A factory was being constructed near the coast. Someone who transports materials to that factory regularly could have stolen this gun. Or anybody escaping from

Sri Lanka refugee camp could have stolen this. Or somebody could have wanted to teach a lesson to duty constables by stealing this. I thought over the matter. But there was no refugee camp nearby nor could a long gun be carried for a long distance without people noticing it. I concluded probably the last reasoning could be correct.

We arranged for a vehicle fitted with mike and loudspeakers and informed people in the villages in 20 miles circumference area about the loss of gun and warned that if anyone has taken it, the same could be left in a public place, else severe action would follow. Not only that, we got hold of drivers who were transporting a number of articles to the factory site and made inquiries. Policemen were also pressed into service in Tirukkadaiyur to search for the gun. In the evening and during night the search went on. I was staying in a lodge near the famous temple. By 9.00 p.m. all the shops had been closed. I had to have food by 3.00 am. in the morning so that fasting could continue during daytime. At that time the temple chief priest voluntarily came forth and told me that he would prepare breakfast and would bring. I told him that I would have bread and plantain and refused his offer. But he said nothing doing and brought sharply at 3.00 in the morning a Tiffin-carrier. When I opened it had hot idlis, vadas, sambhar, coconut and tomato chutney, chilly powder with ghee and all! I expressed by hearty gratitude. But he said that when I had gone over to their place, was keeping awake throughout the night and before fasting in the day time had to eat something early in the morning, it was the minimum he could do and that if that was not done there was no sense in being human beings at all. I told him that here is where we find human value cutting across religion and caste. If this attitude had been with everyone there would not have been demolition of Babri Masjid and as a consequence serial blasts in Mumbai.

Around 6 in the morning, despite Margazhi cold, a 70 year old woman had gone to a nearby tank along with her two grand daughters. The children dipped their legs in the water and said it was very cold and reached the top steps. The grandmother said, "Look, I don't feel cold" and dipped into the water. While taking bath she stumbled on some thing hard and found out the gun. When I was in the check-post the old woman came there in drenched clothes along with grand daughters and informed me about it. I went there and retrieved the gun. Gave some presents to the grandmother and the grand daughters. It was obvious that someone must have seen the constable on duty sleeping and in order to teach him a lesson must have taken the gun and thrown that into the tank. That came out in the investigation. The constable was temporarily suspended and a departmental inquiry was also ordered. I was reminded of Poet Pattukkottai Kalyanasundaram's MGR song, "Don't sleep....If one were to sleep during duty, he would lose his job!" How appropriate are the words.

62

Establishing of Civil Police Service in Maldives

Meeting with the Maldives Defence Minister in the year 2000.

The Maldives is a small state but has a cluster of nearly 1,500 small islands. It is off Tiruvananthapuram in the southern direction. Maldives is a beautiful country with plenty of nature's bounties. It attracts visitors from all over the world just for the grand aesthetic scenic beauty. Most of the business done there is in American dollars only. As many people from Western countries come, narcotics also is smuggled into that place and sold there. There is an Army to provide security to the people. Even the responsibility of maintaining internal law and order belonged to Army only. Some years back, an opposition party leader wanted to capture power there with the help of Tamil militants in Sri Lanka. But that attempt was foiled with the help of Indian Navy.

It was then seriously thought that for the maintenance of internal law and order and prevention of crimes a civil police service must be formed. The Government of India appointed a Goodwill Committee in which ADGP of Sardar Vallabhbhai Academy in Hyderabad, Mr. Prasad and I were members and sent us to Maldives during the year 2000. We reached Tiruvananthapuram and from there after 30 minutes' flight reached Maldives. We held discussions with the Defence Minister and higher officials. Whenever military personnel regulate the traffic there, they wear an overcoat with the legend "We are Police" and do their duty. When we went there was a five-nation foot-ball competition in which national teams of India, Nepal, Srilanka, Bangladesh and Maldives participated. To control the fans of football, the army personnel had an overcoat besides their uniform with the legend "Police". In Maldives no permission is given for strike or demonstration or procession. They took us in a boat to an island where people indulging in narcotic smuggling, consumption etc. were confined. They are not detained there for more than three months. It appeared as if they also spend their time there as tourists.

One Friday I went to the main mosque there and participated in Juma Kutba(congregational prayers). The President of the Maldives Janab Abdul Kayum had also come there on that day. After the prayers, he shook hands with people who had assembled without any fuss. When he came near where was standing, he shook hands with me and made special enquiries

about us. It did not look as if we were meeting the Head of a State but the simplicity made us feel as if we were talking to one of Our Panchayat Union leaders. There was absolutely no ostentation.

ADGP Mr.Prasad and I were there for three days finalising discussions on arrangements for the formation of civil police service. After returning to India, we also submitted a report to the Government of India.

63

Pilgrimage to Mecca on Official Duty

I was S.P. Coastal Security Group in 1999. I was selected to go on official duty to select the buildings for the stay of Indian who perform Haj. What is Haj? One must know of it. Kabaa, the symbol of monotheism, theory of one god, was built by Prophet Ibrahim (Abraham) at Mecca. Later on the structure was developed by Prophet Mohamed. Even to-day the footprints of Prophet Ibrahim are preserved in an enclosure. Prophet Abraham bore the brunt of humiliation from his clan for teaching One God theory. He was driven away by the men of his tribe leaving his wife and son Ismail in his tender age. His wife was searching water by wandering between hillocks Sava and Marva without any success. Surprisingly a spring came out under the feet of infant Ismail. The spring was later on called as Zam Zam, which quenches the thirst of lakhs of pilgrims and became perennial.

Subsequently Prophet Mohamed started teachings of One God "Allah" theory after getting the revelation. He was put into humiliation and physical torture. He was driven from Mecca to Medina which is 450 miles away. His theory was accepted in Medina. He along with his followers came back to Mecca and outnumbered the opponents by way of his preachings. His journey to Mecca and performing other rituals are called as Haj. The muslims all over the world perform the Haj since it is their fourth obligations, apart from reciting of Kalima (basic tenets), prayer, fasting and zakat (alms to poor).

I was curious to see the holy places since I studied Islamic History in my post-graduation. I took my wife along with me. We reached Jeddah by catching Saudi Airlines. We were received by the Indian consulate officials at the airport. I called on the Consul-General, Mr. Afzal Ammanullah, IAS, who had given warm welcome and briefed the duties. After a brief meeting we left to Mecca in the night itself and we performed umrah (religious duties at Kabaa) on reaching there. We were accommodated a lodge behind the Indian Dy. Consul Office.

Next morning I reported to Dy. Consul. He described elaborately about the judging of buildings based on the distance from Haram, amenities like kitchen, toilets, floor space, movement area, and escalator facilities and so on. I was given two assistants for the work. I had done duties for 21 days. I was really astonished to see basically an arid hillock surrounded Mecca became international renowned hub by the visit of lakhs of pilgrims every year. By wearing the white clothes for performing umrah, it is shown to the mankind that we are going to reach the grave yard one day what ever position we possess in the earth. To expound the philosophy, I was shown the grave yard and I was astonished to see no beautification of any grave, whether they were the kith and kin of Prophet or King of Saudi Arabia or any dignitary. All are given simple burial and no symbolic presence of their graves. We have not seen any picture, art, and sculpture anywhere in the city. People are forbidden to hero worship, which is a contrast to many countries.

Strikingly Madina is a green place full of date palms, gardens and oasis. It is in Madina Prophet Mohamed is buried. There also no one is allowed to raise their hands in praise of Prophet.

I saw 'Laden Company' doing construction work. It struck me the name associated with Bin Laden. When I enquired my cousin Dr.Ajmal who was working in the Govt. Hospital for 15 years along with his wife Dr. Sulaika, told me that the company belonged to Bin Laden Family. He showed me the palace of Bin Lade, which resembles like our Raj Bhavan. I was informed that all the kith and kin of Osama Bin Laden are peace loving and busy business people. I pity on Osama for his misadventure instead of leading peaceful life.

During the course of selecting the building I came across an interesting incident. One morning an old Arab woman aged 70 along with her 30 year son came to Dy. Consul Office and requested him to inspect her building for the rent. On his direction I along with the other staff visited her 3 storey old building. On inspection I found that there were no sufficient toilets and kitchen. I wrote the report that the building was not suitable. After 10 days I saw that old lady alone sitting in front of Dy. Consul. She pleaded with him that she had made additional facilities of toilets and kitchen and told him that it was her source of income. Dy. Consul had also requested me to inspect again on compassionate ground.

I again went to her house along with the staff. I found her 30 old son sitting on the ground. The old woman struggled through the steps to show the added facilities. When I enquired her about her son, she said with a long sigh that her son got married with a Palestinian bride by giving heavy money. Since there was no employment for her son, her daughter-in-law went away to Palestine. From then onward her son was mentally upset. She told me that the rental income from the building was her only income. Taking pity on her I gave the note of selecting the building. This was not the one case. Many Arabs rented out their buildings during Hajj times and live in luxurious life in Western countries having foreigners as wives. So the poor Arabs remain poor without getting proper employment. The bride grooms have to give heavy Sheridan to their brides and many people remain till the age of 30.

I could see that taxis used to fleece the pilgrims as usual in all pilgrim centres. I found that the shops including the jewellery shops left unlocked when the call for the prayer (Aazan) given. I could see that some Africans begging with one hand. On enquiry I came to know that their hands were cut off because they committed thefts. The beggars are being chased with whips.

After finishing the work I submitted a note to Consul General at Jeddah and I got commendation from him.

64

The Story of Suppressing Caste Violence Through Sticks and Love

The present Cuddalore and Villuppuram districts in those days were an integrated South Arcot District. Puducherry Union territory lies in between these districts. If South Arcot was a British fort, Puducherry was a French fortress. People in this place are largely Vanniars and Adi Dravidars. In physique you won't find much distinction between these two castes. But in economic power, the Vanniars were the dominant caste. Adi Dravidars were the wage-earners under the Vanniars. Adi Dravidars were a suppressed caste for several hundreds of years. In the recent times, due to awakening of social consciousness among them by great Freedom fighter-Congressman like Ilaiya Perumal, the youngsters in Adhi Diravida community are now prepared to fight for their fundamental rights.

In 1985 I was working as Additional S.P. and Mr. Radhakrishnaraju as the S.P. of South Arcot District. In Kattumannargudi of Chidambaram Taluq, a caste clash was in the offing. In the local festival, Adi Dravidars were pleasing the crowd with beating of the drums. The Vanniyar youth in its exuberance in seeing the dance and hearing the drums, threw coins on the Adi Dravidar girls who were dancing. When their actions were objected to, they beat up the dancing party of Adi Drvidars. When the news spread all the Adi Dravidar agricultural labourers stopped the work. This went to the extent of big clashes and police firing. When Adi Dravdars wanted to return to work, the landlords refused to take them back. This led to further disharmony. Huts and haystacks were burnt. The S.P. and I camped in Kattumannargudi and brought the situation under control.

In June 2000, from AIG in DGP Office, I was promoted D.I.G. Home Guards. Mr. Abhai Kumar Singh was the S.P. of Cuddalore District and Mr.Ravi was the S.P. of Villupuram District. Mr.Bolonath, IG Armed Reserve, was also holding Additional charge of DIG, Villupuram. In the third week of June, Vanniar-Adi Dravidar communal violence broke out and everywhere there were arson, looting, burning of huts, haystacks, etc. The violence spread to the whole of Cuddalore and Villupuram districts. Mr.Govind, ADGP Social Security was sent there to oversee law and order problem. I was sent to assist the I.G. Mr. Bolonath. When I reached Cuddalore, I was asked to proceed to Nellikkuppam. Only the preceding day many Vanniar and Adi Dravidar houses had been burnt. In fact when I reached there, many houses were still burning. The miscreants were hiding in sugar cane fields in and around Nellikkuppam. Whenever there was no police patrol, these miscreants would come out, set fire to huts, homes and go back to their hiding places. When I went there, I formed different groups of constables and sent them to different directions to go after the miscreants who were hiding in sugar cane fields. We arrested a number of mischief mongers. After this round-up I did not allow the constables to return home and relax. I made them continuously engage in patrolling and along with them I also sat on the benches which were placed on street junctions consecutively for three days and nights. In all these days shops had been closed. My Presidency College mate Abu Salih, a native of Nellikuppam arranged food for me and all the constables from his house. When Mr. Govind came to Nellikkuppam, he saw me seated in the middle of the road junction and complimented me.

Display of burnt bus in inter-caste violence

Thereafter, there were unpleasant incidents in Kumaratchi, Kattu Mannargudi, Pennadam, Thittakkudi and Sethiathope. Some buses were also burnt. I visited those places then and there along with Salem I.G. Mr. Jegannathan, Mr. Sailendra Babu and Mr. Arunachalam, SP. and took stern action. When under the leadership of Minister Mr. M.R.K. Panner Selvam an all-party meeting was held at Cuddalore, I participated in it on behalf of Mr. Bholonath, IG.

Mr. Bholonath, IGP wrote a letter to DGP Mr. Sharma requesting to be relived of the responsibilities of DIG Villuppuram. On the latter's recommendation, Mr. Sekar, Joint Commissioner of Police, Traffic, was appointed as DIG Villupuram on 27.6.2000. But as he went on medical leave, he was put in charge of Home Guards, DIG and I was appointed as the D.I.G. Villupuram. I took charge of the post on 30.6.2000A.N.

விழுப்புரம் சரக டி.ஐ.ஜி.,யாக நியமிக்கப்பட்ட முகமது அலி நேற்று கடலூரில் பொறுப்பேற்றார். அவரிடம் ஐ.ஜி., போலோநாத் பொறுப்புகளை ஒப்படைத்தார்.

Thereafter my lightning actions started. The Tamil Proverbs say, "He who wields baton, is the Chief.", "Nothing will help as inflicting a dose of beating". I encouraged the constables in the both the districts. Then I got into proactive steps: saw to it that there was intense patrolling in the affected areas. Wherever there were incidents of stone-throwing, burning of vehicles or arson we rushed there and caught hold of criminals and put them in prison. People who blocked the roads were then and there arrested. Once when some people blocked the vehicle of Minister Panner Selvam, we arranged for the passage to be cleared. 87 cases were registered in connection with communal clashes and 139 people were arrested in Cuddalore district and 119 in Villupuram district by the swift action.

Conducting raid against illicit distillation at Jayankondapattinam by crossing the sea backwater in a boat.

I learnt that the respective caste leaders were instigating the violence from behind the scenes. At a meeting held in Cuddalore, Vazhapadi Ramamoorthy, a congress leader stated that Vanniar Sangha president and Dalit Peravai president were instigating violence. (Dinamalar, 13.7.2000). Under a measure putting the trouble shooters behind the bar 15 persons booked under preventive detention and 30 people were arrested under Goonda Act. The Chief Minister M.Karunanidhi announced that whoever indulges in caste violence would be arrested under Preventive Detention Act. The Government also warned through newspapers that in Villupuram and Cuddalore districts whoever indulged in violence would be arrested. (Thina Thanthi, 14.10.2000).

Another important reason for caste violence could be attributed to the prevalence of brewing illicit liquor, sale of the same, smuggling etc. There were some who indulge in brewing illicit liquor in the interior sugarcane fields, rose gardens, cashew nut groves, coconut groves, etc. become emboldened to beat up people belonging to both the castes. The raw material required for illicit brewing, molasses is available in a number of places there where there are sugar-cane crushing centres. Similarly in Senchi Kalvarayan hills area also illicit brewing went on. They were then brought to the neighbouring districts of Cuddalore and Villuppuram through smuggling. With this income they were meeting the expenses involved in the cases against communal violence. Therefore, all the police officials were brought together, a week was declared as Prevention of Illicit liquor Week. (Thina Thanthi, July 20, 2000). Kilwanikuppam, Hilkundalavadi, Nellikkuppam, Naduvirappattu, Karunagaranallu,Pennadam,Vallampadugai, Jeyengonda-pattinam, Sammattipuram, Thiagavalli in Cuddalore District, Kalvarayan range Kodamuritti, Kallanatham, Nagakuppam, Tirukkoilur Murugambadi in Villupuram District were all personally raided by me and we seized lakhs worth liquor, pots which were hidden in cement tanks and barrels and destroyed them. Hundreds of persons involved in illicit brewing of liquor were arrested and their activities were put an end to.

The next step was visiting each village and getting villagers' pledge to abolish brewing and consumption of liquor. In Sammattipuram, Cuddalore, Minister M.R.K. Panner Selvam also participated in the meeting. The cultural programme of the students of Vadalur Vallalar High School on abolition of liquor was appreciated by everyone. Not stopping with that, rehabilitation assistance was given by the banks through the recommendation of the District Collector for those who had given up illicit brewing.

65

A Peaceful Procession for Eradication of Violence

Peace march at Villupuram.

The first target that comes to the minds of those who indulge in violence and demonstrations is the government buses. The government has taken pains to serve people in even interior villages by providing bus services. But those anti-social elements stop these buses, force the passengers to get down and burn the buses and run away from the place. Innocent public with their bag and baggage and children have to reach their destinations in day time or during night after facing great difficulties. To teach a lesson to such iron hearted violence-mongers, transport officials, college principals, school heads and government officials conducted a meeting and it was decided to point out to the instigators of caste violence the enormity of their wickedness by organising Peace Processions. In this procession, focus should be on abolition of caste and stress on man's brotherhood and fraternity. The buses burnt during the agitations should also be paraded. It was also decided to utilise students' cultural shows to focus on abolition of violence, brewing of illicit liquor etc. by effective propaganda.

All the buses that were damaged during violence were pressed into service for 'Peace Procession'. (Dinamalar, 25.10.2000). The Peace Procession started from Ramakrishna Higher Secondary School, Villupuram on 17.10.2000. The atmosphere wore a festive look. Mr.G.Vasudevan, Govt. Transport Villupuram Division General Manager, Mr. Ilangovan, District Educational Officer, Mr. Ravi and Mr. Davidson, the two District S.Ps., all participated in the function. The procession went via Kolianur, Panruti, Cuddalore, Kullanchavadi, Kumaratchi and Sethiarthope and terminated at Vadalore on November 19th 2000. Without distinction of caste or religion it was welcomed by people on the route. It became apparent that people want a peaceful life only and shun at communal and caste violence. Only a handful of mischief mongers indulge in violence. Also they had come to the conclusion that unity alone would pave the way for a good life. It is to be mentioned that after this, there were no major caste violence's in Cuddalore district.

In appreciation of my services in the Police Department, the President of India's Gold Medal for Meritorious service was announced on Independence Day, 2000.

President Police Medal winners

(Clockwise) Ms. Lotika Saran, IPS, IG, Directorate of Vigillance and Anti-Corruption (DVAC), was awarded the President Police Medal for Distinguished service. Mr. A.P. Mohammed Ali, IPS, was awarded with the President Police Medal for Meritorious Service. Mr. P.S. Sethuraman, Dy. SP, DVAC, Chennai was awarded with the President Police Medal for Meritorious Service, Mr. C. Vivekanandan, Inspector, DVAC, Coimbatore, was awarded with the President Police Medal for Meritorious Service.

In a letter DT. 24.8.2000 Mrs.Sheela Priya, Secretary to the Governor, Ms.Fathima Beevi, sent Greetings on behalf of the Governor for getting the Presidential award. News regarding this was published in the following papers: Dina Bhoomi, 17.8.2000, Dinamani 16.8.2000, Thiina Thanthi 20.8.2000, Malai Malar, Dinamani 17, 18.11.2000, Dinamalar 19.11.2000, Dinamalar, 18.11.2000, Thina Thanthi 18.11.2000.)

In its 19th September 2000 issue, on page 5, Dinamani under the caption "Peace returns to Cuddalore and Villupuram" published a report. I view it as a satisfactory appraisal.

Mr.Jeeva Murgesan, Organising Secretary of Human Brotherhood Centre, Neyveli wrote a letter to me on 19.11.2000. It states, "The concluding function of Peace March at Vadalore on 18.11.2000 was very impressive...You participated in the meeting and gave a great speech on Brotherhood of Humanity.

The way you described the rain that poured too had its meaningful significance. Your noble sentiments and the concern you have for the welfare of all, were appreciated by everyone in the crowd. In brief, the speech was a fitting finale of the Peace Procession."

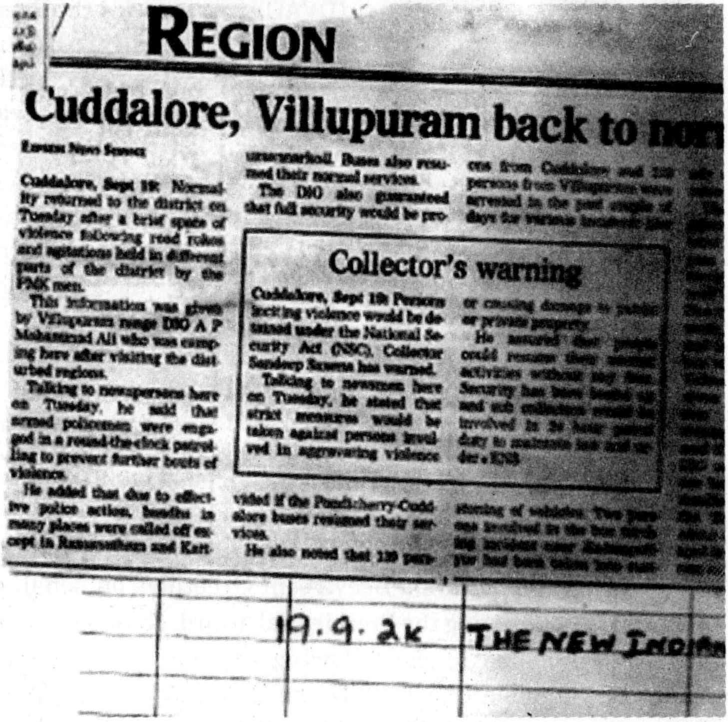

REGION

Cuddalore, Villupuram back to nor[mal]

Collector's warning

19.9.2K THE NEW INDIA[N]

Mrs. Vasundara Devi, a member of the State General Council of Pattali Makkal Katchi in a letter DT. 20.11.2000 stated, "I have learnt with great joy through newspaper reports your timely and correct action against rowdies without caste and religious distinction. For women like me who were worrying whether there would be no end to this rowdyism, your actions call for great appreciation. I pray that your straightforward, responsible actions without being afraid of any political interference will continue in future as well."

Similarly Kottagam Panchayat Union leader in Neyveli Mr.G. Jayaraman wrote in a letter, "My village and Sammattikkuppam are bound by many relations. Still it was a fact that as some in that village were dealing with illicit liquor, we had disliked entering into matrimonial alliance with those people. You have made it very clear through students' cultural programmes that neither power nor order could remove this evil and that people should have change of hearts to lead a good life. Your message that this illicit liquor menace could be put an end with cooperation and goodwill of all deserves our gratitude."

66

Sharpen Your Intelligence, not the Knife

While I was serving as D.I.G. Villupuram in 2000, one day I was returning from Panrutti to Villupuram by car. A jeep overtook my car, about 12 youth in the car were making much noise and tapping the vehicles that were plying; their jeep did not have a registration number at the backside. I asked my driver to follow the jeep. When we entered into Villupuram Police jurisdiction, I asked the driver to overtake the vehicle and stop the same. It had a number plate at the front. The flag of Vanniar Sangham was fluttering.

I asked them all to get down and began to inquire about their whereabouts. They said they were coming from Kaduvetti area of Perambalur District and as P.M.K. leader was proceeding to Tirunelveli by train, they were also going there to give security to him throughout his tour. We checked the vehicle. A big cloth sack was full of Veechu Arivals : We also found heavy casuarina sticks.

We took them to Villupuram along with the weapons. A case was registered against them. Some prominent people in Villupuram including an M.L.A. of P.M.K. came to meet me. I told them that it was the responsibility of the Police to give protection to important leaders and advised them that it was not proper to send their party cadre with weapons for that purpose. In politics there could be ideological differences but not that of the clashes of weapons. How appropriate the poet had stated, "Don't sharpen swords but sharpen your intelligence!"

67

Recovery of Stolen Goods–Returned to Owners–Appreciation of Police

The Police take up responsibility of not only protecting the lives of the people but their properties as well. It should recover goods that have been stolen and duly returned the same to the rightful owners. By doing so, the Police department would earn a good name. After rescuing Villupuram and Cuddalore districts from a detériorating Law and Order situation, to prevent crimes occurring, we increased night patrolling and also monitor the work of the police during nights. We compiled a list of criminals and formed separate squads to restore the recovered stolen goods. The recovered goods thus were returned to the owners in Villupuram on 25.9.2000 (Malai Malar 26.9.2000, Thina Thanthi 28.9.2000, Dinamalar 27.9.2000) and at Neyveli on 10.10.2000 (Malai Malar 11.10.2000, Thina Thanthi 12.10.2000, Indian Express 11.10.2000).

The District Armed Force forms the backbone of Police in every district. Because during any emergency it will swing into swift action. We arranged for a function to felicitate those did exemplary service in Cuddalore and Villupuram. Constables

were complimented and prizes distributed. By this 'morale boosting' the Police force functioned efficiently in Cuddalore and Villupuram districts.

68

Uthirapathi Changes as 'Vetri' – Setback in Rescuing Kannada Actor Rajukumar

Everybody knows the story of how Kannada Actor Rajukumar was abducted along with two others by sandalwood smuggler Veerappan in 2000 and how the whole of Tamil Nadu and Karnataka was agitated over this and later due to the efforts of leader Pazha.Nedumaran, Prof. Kalyani and Tindivanam Sukumar he was rescued. But not many know how the Tamil Nadu Police missed the rare opportunity of rescuing Rajukumar.

Uthirapathi (28) was the son of Veerakumar who belonged to Senninatham village within the jurisdiction of Sethiathope Police Station in Cuddalore. Delta Party which was monitoring the activities of Tamil Vidulai group (Militant Outfit) in Cuddalore District arrested him on suspicion when he came to visit his sister who was in hospital. During the investigation some shocking revelations emerged. The S.P. of the District informed me about the same and I too went there and got acquainted with the details.

Uthirapathi stopped his school education in the middle and was running a tea-shop in Senninatham. Lenin and Maran who belonged to Tamizhar Viduthalai. Group would come to his shop for drinking tea. One Chinnathambi had introduced them to Uthirapathi and had told that if he too joined Tamizhar Viduthalai group, he would get good money. He was admitted into the group in 1993. This group had attacked Kullanchavadi Police Station in Cuddalore District.

Thereafter this group along with an extremist Ilavarasan of Andimadam area had intensely propagated extremist views in many villages. But as Ilavarasan got involved in many Kattapanchayat incidents (Kangaroo court) differences of opinion cropped up. Maran and Radio Venkatesan began to function as a separate group. The extremist groups in the Andimadam area split into two: Coovagam Ramasamy and Ilavarasan headed the groups. After Ramasamy was murdered, there were many murders in both the groups. Seeing that Andimadam Police Station could not prevent these murders, Maran and under his leadership Venkatesan, Natarajan and Ponnivalavan attacked Andimadam Police Station and decamped with 5 guns, a revolver and many bullets. They were involved in some robberies and thereafter got in touch with Sandalwood smuggler Veerappan. The Maran group integrated with Veerappan. Uthirapathi and one Meghanathan were taken to Veerapan on 23.6.2000. There were about 15 people with Veerappan. As Uthirapathi was indisposed he left to see his sister who was getting treated in Chidambaram; on 26.7.2000 he had started from Talavadi in Coimbatore District. When he came to Chidambaram he was intercepted by the Delta Police Party. Kannada Actor Rajukumar had been kidnapped three days after Uthirapathi had left Veerappan. The governments of Tamil Nadu and Karnataka were jointly making efforts to trace him. I and Cuddalore S.P. told the I.G. Law and Order and ADGP whatever information conveyed by Uthirapathi. The I.G. Law & Order asked us to keep a Special squad and said that he would inform us after talking with DGP. After some time the I.G. phoned me up and said that the DGP wanted me to meet him. I also met him accordingly. He asked me to give into writing the details furnished by Uthirapathi and that he would be closeted with Karnataka I.G. (CID) and asked me to wait in the office. After two hours he came to his office with a drenched face and told me that I could get back to my headquarters in Villupuram. I passed on this information to I.G. and ADGP and returned to Villupuram. In a couple of days Uthirapathi was asked to be handed over to Sivaganga District Police for some investigation. Thereafter Sivaganga Police investigated him. Then STF took over and Uthirapathi alias Vetri was remanded into custody on a suspicion case. Politics seems to have played its game in converting Uthirapathi into Vetri. A chance was lost to locate Veerappan and it was also unfortunate that many more months had to elapse before Actor Rajukumar could be rescued after paying heavy sums.

69

A Rare Meeting with a Convict in a Double-Murder Case

On 2nd June 1993, in the evening a group of four riff-raff youth had entered into a hotel in Waltax Road, Chennai and attempted to drink liquor there. The hotel owner's son Nissar and an employee of the hotel Nasimuddin tried to stop this. The group refused to listen to their entreaties and attempted to consume liquor. The employee Nasimuddin tried to seize the liquor bottle. All the four attacked Nasimuddin with knives, killed him and ran away from the place. They had come to Mint bus stop which was 2km away and then got into a bus proceeding to Broadway. When the bus was nearing the theatre they had trodden on the leg of a passenger Yusuf. When Yusuf remonstrated, they killed him by attacking with the knives and escaped from the place.

As both the murdered were Muslims, it was feared that there could be some communal clash. Immediately I, Assistant Commissioners Mr. Ramasubramani and Mr. Sivaprakasam reached the area and investigated the background of assailants, the possible reasons for the murders etc. Our investigation revealed that there was absolutely no prior enmity between the victims-murdered and the assailants. While we were making inquiries in Broadway, we came to know that 1.Leftjohn, 2. Amalraj, 3. Thakkaliraja of New Washermenpet and 4. Maya of Mannadi Krishnan were involved in this.

We arrested them on that night itself. The murderers were young. On investigation they said that they had done so under the influence of liquor. I said, "Why have you behaved so stupidly under the influence of liquor, murdering some people and without caring for the family responsibility going to prison as well? You could at least have earned a decent living by plying cycle rickshaw!" At that time the assembly session was going on. The then DGP Mr. Sripal contacted me early in the morning and learnt about the details of double murder and the reasons. I explained in detail and said that this was not due to any religious violence and the murders were solely done under the influence of intoxication. Mr.Sripal said that the Leader of the Opposition Mr. S.R. Balasubramaniam wanted to know the full details and asked me to explain full details to him. Accordingly I talked to Mr. S.R. Balasubramaniam and acquainted him with full details and how the criminals have been arrested. He was satisfied. Thereafter the case was conducted and the Hon'ble Court convicted them for life-term.

After my retirement, in 2007 February, I was attending to some minor repairs in my residence at Kotwal Chavadi. One Anandan, the carpenter brought some wooden articles in a cycle rickshaw from Mannadi. After unloading the articles in my home he said that the rickshaw driver wanted to meet me. I asked him whether he had paid the loading charges and why the rickshaw driver wanted to meet me. He said he had paid him the fare but the rickshaw driver insisted on seeing me. I asked him to bring him to my room in the upstairs. He was about 40 and very lean. He asked whether I recognised him. I said I could not trace him. He said that I arrested him in the double murder case in 1993. He had earned a good name in prison and heeding to my advice has been plying cycle rickshaw, doing an honest job. I advised him to continue in the honest path and protect his family. It is clear from the above incident that when a man commits crime due to circumstances and punished by law, he could atone for his fault and turn a new leaf in his life!

70

Violation of Human Rights- Some Incidents of Human- Itarian Nature in the Prison

As D.I.G C.B.C.I.D Leading Tamil Nadu State Police Team for All India Police Duty Meet at Banglore 2003.

"Save Police Officials from the politicians!", "Save police constables from the politicians!" These were the slogans raised by none other than Mr.C.V. Narasimhan and Mr.V.R. Lakshminarayanan, who were Directors of CBI, CBI Reuben and other Lawyers and Human Rights Associations. The above slogans rented the air in a meeting of Human Rights activists on 16.3.2007. This was reported in Deccan Chronicle, page 5, 16.3.2007. As I had arrested Kalaignar M. Karunadhi in connection with Chennai fly-over cases, I, too, was made a sacrifical lamb by the politicians. By suitable amendment to Indian Police Act which was framed by the Britishers in 1861, ways and means must be found to stop politicians wreak vengeance on the officials by stretching law in their favour and make it their hand maid.

State Police Duty Meet held on 27-6-2003 at Chennai

As per Semmozhi Mootharijnar's words, "If you get up before the Cock' calls, you can even boldly encounter a lion", on 1.7.2004 around 5.30 in the morning I partook a glass of warm water in which a spoonful of honey had been mixed. As usual at 5.45 a.m. with baton in my hands, shoulders squared up and eyes piercing straight ahead I started my usual morning walk from my official residence in Taylor's Road, Kilpalk and proceeded via Ormes Road, Sylvan Colony, Burnaby Road, Landon's Road and finished morning walk and returned home by 6.30 a.m., perspiring after the brisk walk. I did some Yoga for some time. Then from the perspiring clothes changed into lungi. My wife had brought a cup of hot coffee, which I started sipping slowly. Around 7 O'clock, my wife informed me that after ringing the calling bell thrice, finding the doors open, four or five people had come inside the hall and were standing. I put on my shirt and reached the hall from the room. One Mr. S.P. Kapoor introduced himself as from CBI and said he wanted to search my house.

I was arrested on 1.7.2004. On 2.7.2004, I, Mr. Sankar, A.C. and Mr. Sadu, an L.I.C. officer were produced before Addl.C.M.M. I/c. Ms. Alamelu's Court in the so called Stamp racket scams.

We were in police custody for 3 days. Thereafter we were taken to Chennai Central Jail on the evening of 5.7.2004. We were entrusted to the care of Addl.Superintendent by CBI officers. The Addl. S.P. Mr. Govindaraj questioned them 'where was the personal identification memo'. The CBI officer Karamyal said they did not know anything about that: they had entrusted the remanded. People to their care and they must care of the next. The Addl. S.P. calmly pointed out the Jail Manual and firmly told that they must have brought the memo from the magistrate. He said that he would take us any way but in future the CBI people must follow it strictly. I was reminded of Tamil literary saying, "Even if you open you third eye to reduce me to ashes, a mistake is a mistake."

When I was Vannarapettai A.C. and then North Chennai D.C. Law and Order I had come to the Central Prison many times. In 1980 when I was AC, in connection with an agitation I had taken from the Central prison former minister Nanjil Manoharan, D.M.K. Chennai District Secretary, Mr.R.D.

Sitapathy, Mr. M.K. Stalin, present minister to Egmore and Saidapet courts. When I crossed the threshold of the same jail, as a prisoner I was naturally put out. We were taken straight away to quarantine cell. The prison official who took us to quarantine cell pointed out that in a particular cell the former Chief Minister and the present Chief Minister had been confined. In front of that cell there was a pipal tree. There was a small temple for Pillayar. Nearby was a coconut tree. We were told that particular coconut tree as a sapling had been planted by former Chief Minister, Ms. Jayalalitha.

The building we were confined was constructed during the British days. When I was there for five days it rained. The rainwater drenched the bed. The biting from the mosquitoes coming from dirty Cooum River and the stink emanating from the river will make people shudder to come to jail again. But there are many jailbirds who bear that and come to this prison many times.

A prisoner, Murthy from Cuddappah waited for someone to take him out on bail but for two months nobody had turned up. One evening he was standing before Vinayakar temple and was abusing God. I asked him why he was doing so. He said two months had elapsed since his arrest and nobody had come forward still to bail him out. I asked what God could do anything when his brothers and relations did not bother. On some other occasion at the door step he placed his head and was crying. I consoled him. Thereafter in five days' time when he got bail, he hurriedly left the place even without informing Vinayakar.

Relatives would come to see the prisoners in jail. Sometimes there would be heart-rending scenes. Once when we were taken from the jail to the Court, a woman with a babe-in-arms saw her husband and was about to return. The small baby wanted to go near the father and cried. On some other occasion a TADA Prisoner told his wife who had come to see him, "Pray to God! Even though I have been in prison for seven years, God has not shown mercy still!" One could gauge the depth of his feelings. But there were some prisoners who were very happy! The reason was they were looked after very well after greasing on the palms of the jail officials. Even when jail birds leave prison, they are in touch with the officials.

I knew that illicit brewing of liquor could be absolutely wiped out: but I also learnt that the reason for that not happening was the encouragement given by some policemen. Such policemen suggest ways and means not only for brewing but for distribution and other associated activities. Those prisoners who were serving term for illicit brewing explained that the only way to meet the expenses in the Police Stations was to get the illegal gratification from those brewing illicit liquor. Whenever a serious raid is contemplated, it meant increase in the amount given to the constables. That is why the Tamil Nadu Chief Minister MGR decided to introduce selling bottled liquor. Those who bid for such shops had their own private force to detect and wipe out illicit brewing. One such bidder in Chennai had not paid the revenues to the Govt. for months together because of his closeness with political higher-up and established a big hospital and medical college with that illegal revenue. But when the government itself sells through its outlet liquor, illicit liquor brewing goes on and those police who indirectly encourage it have a field day during Deepavali time.

When my elder daughter in Saudi Arabia heard about by arrest she came to Chennai along with her children to be with her mother who otherwise would have lived alone. Usually when my grandchildren come I used to take them to Marina Beach, Guindy Children's Park, Vandaloor zoo etc. On 5.7.2004 my six-year old grandson when he came to Chennai immediately asked where "Nanna"' (Grandfather) was (That is how he used to address me). My daughter had said that I had gone to office. Till evening as I had not returned home, my daughter had told him that I was in jail. That night he had woken up twice or thrice and had cried. Next morning my daughter came to meet me in jail along with my grandson and my wife.

He was brought to the visitors' section by the authorities. He came with great affection but began to cry aloud worrying whether he too would be put in the cage. He was taken out and left with my daughter outside. When he was in Saudi, he used to dress himself as a Police Officer and used to say that he would become like Nanna(me) and brandished a baton too. Now when he saw the cages in prison and the dresses of the wardens, he became much afraid. When children see their beloved in prison, they are deeply affected. The prisoners also learn how much they are beholden to the family members. Mr. Sankar, AC who was arrested along with me, has a daughter who was born several years after his marriage. She was studying in the seventh standard. When his wife came to meet him she did not bring the girl. Once the girl was also brought along and after they had left Mr.Sankar was in a despondent mood and it took a great deal of time and energy to bring him back to normalcy.

Cats and bandicoots move with great agility during night time in large numbers. One day when I was in deep sleep, there was some noise. I woke up and found that cat was moving out with a plastic bag in which bread pieces were there. Then after some time I asked the Superintendent I/c. Mr.Rajendran whether wire mesh could be provided to prevent rats, bandicoots and cats from sprawling the place all over. He said he had made such provision for the former Chief Minister Jayaalitha and subsequently had to face the consequence in the form of transfer to a remote sub-jail; the implication was that he would not do anything.

In three months of prison life, I also wrote some poems and kaana songs. I could read a number of books. Rober Schuller's "Success is Never Ending, Failure Is Never Final"and "Tough times never last, but tough people do," Kannadasan's Raththa Pushpangal, Omar Khayam's poems, Na Kamaraja's Santhosha Kanavugal, Moovendar's Sudar Vilakku, Kumari Anandan's Kaduvlai Nokki, Dr. Alagukkannan's "Culture and Social Hisotry as depicted in

Silappadikaram"and some more. At 4.30 a.m. the mosque from the nearby Periamedu would proclaim the call of the muzzain: I would then finish morning prayers fajar. Within the cell I would do some exercises and yoga practices. Then the doors would be opened for taking roll-call. This is how even a prison cell became my living place for 90 days. By victimising a higher police officer by fixing up a case to take a revenge will deter the other officers from carrying out the official duties because the politicians who were happy for my detention in central prison had openly thundered in the public meetings that the fate which had befallen on me would also follow if any officer took action against them. Hence the rights of human beings are violated openly by administering such open threats.

POEMS WRITTEN IN A PRISON YARD

On Chennai Central Prison

Many people of varied and curious background
Had sojourned to the confines of Chennai Central Prison;
No distinction of rich and poor, master or servant
Strange it is that I too was for a while in the same prison!

Opposite the buzz of Central Station

For all to behold from the buzz of Central Station
For all to behold the stiniking unkempt Cooum
For all to behold the flight of Flying Trains
For all to behold the plethora of tarred roads

High Walls of the Prison
Over the high compound walls of the prison
Fences firmly charged with electricity
What would befall on a prisoner attempting to escape?
Ask the Warder with lathi to answer the question!

At the Dusk

Inmates will be rounded up in closed cells
Will be exposed to mosquito bite
Throughout the night!
At dawn by six the doors of the cells opened
Ritual of Roll call followed by
Disciplined and measured serving of food
The affluent prisoner will don a fine shirt
The ordinary prisoner will have a numbered one!
Will indulge in arson and violence
Will swindle the public and delight in corrupt
Once put in the Central Prison
Will ask for ac car and air cooler!

Worked hard foregoing food and sleep!

The craftiness of the fox had woven a net
I was pushed into that vile net
A brief period in prison, by God's grace
Converted into an abode of peace

Rickshaw puller's drunken outburst (Kaana Pattu)
Source: Jambu, Kannagi Nagar, Chennai Central Prison inmates

In free verse form: Mohamed Ali

I live by sweating out as a rickshaw puller
Will lose the hard earned money in country liquor
I ply my rickshaw like a rocket
Not even fifty paise is left in my pocket!
Constant pedalling and constant pain in the chest
The body yearns for solace in liquor
Unless 100 ml. is consumed vehicle remains idle
Once consumption of liquor is had, the vehicle flies

Had carefully tucked money to buy sweets for children
A look at liquor shop, the money is gone
Everyday is passed by rickshaw pulling
All the earnings drowned in liquor river!

Man's body nothing but filled up with air (Kaana Pattu)

Source: Jambu, Kannagi Nagar, Chennai Central Prison inmates

In free verse form: Mohamed Ali

Man's life lasts so long as invisible breathing lasts
The way he dances to his whims till his death!
Leads a stingy life but leaves behind property
If the call comes from God, all end as depleted!

Where is the need for rose garlands?
When the legs have been finally stretched!
Man disappears even while sleeping in own bed
Why do you crave for apple swing under the coffin!

Each one will put a garland around, then dance around
Will put a fistful of sand on the mouth, to mark the end!
The body reaches the burning ghat, dirge reaches crescendo!
When once the song is over, would clamour for money!
Even before the sands dry up in the burning ghat!
Relations gather and fight for properties left!
Therefore do not lead a stingy life to leave behind property
All man's dances on earth till only death catches him!

71

American Tour – Some Fascinating Facts

I visited during April-May 2008 United States which is called the world's super power. For two months I had toured there and share with the readers some of my impressions which are very novel. I am sure it would help them to have a better perspective –

Electronic Commerce

The American people do not carry wads of dollar currencies in their purse or bundles of money in bags. Government has given Social Security number for each citizen and exchange of money is done through credit cards. When goods are purchased government credits the amount in the individual's card. Similarly employers credit the money into the credit card account of the employees. If a person uses a credit card without adequate funds in the bank, he would be black listed for seven years. That is for that period he will not be able to buy house, car or any consumer goods by using the credit card.

The use of credit card enables the employers and business organisations to deduct tax payable to government. So tax due from the consumers automatically reaches the government coffers. This prevents circulation of black money. The government also has a number of schemes of social security for retired people, senior citizens, unemployed, disabled, etc., The surplus is utilised for pursuing unnecessary wars like the one against Iraq. In our country also gradually government servants, public sector employees, people who have bank accounts, businessmen who get loans from banks, agriculturists and students are all to be provided with a number with social security credit cards, generation of black money can be abolished. Similarly people who buy goods and do not pay for the same can be blacklisted and such cheatings could be stopped.

Businesses on the principle, If not satisfied, return the goods

The way business is carried on in shops and elsewhere is commendable.

Most of the apparels, electronic goods, toys, etc. are manufactured and imported from China, Japan, Barbados, India, Thailand, Indonesia, Bangladesh, Columbia, etc. On all important holidays and during weekends through internet mail and through letters invitation for buying "sale of goods" is announced carrying 10 to 50 percent discount. People rush towards shops and buy their requirements during those times. They can return the goods if they are not satisfied with the same within a month along with the bill and the shopkeepers take them back. Even if the goods have been used they are taken back. This leads the buyers to again have transactions with the same shop. Shop owners also want customers coming back to them again and again. Not only the customers select the articles, they can also learn price and other details through their computers.

No Cheap, Eyesore Advertisements Anywhere

There is no cheap disfigurement of compound walls of private residential buildings or for that matter public buildings either. Advertisers do not ruin the aesthetic beauty of towns or cities by indiscriminate advertisements. They sometimes request permission from private parties some space and place small placards. They would convey the message of houses for sale or rent, furniture available, sale of consumer goods or any Court orders. These too will be removed in two or three days' time. Sometimes people will be holding aloft advertisement banner on the road side for a few hours: they are paid six to dollars per hour. Otherwise we cannot come across any advertisement glaringly put on the residential walls, on roads or by the roadsides or commercial places, electric posts, etc. We find dustbins specifically provided in residential or commercial blocs. There will be very heavy fine if anything is thrown out indiscriminately on roads or sidewalks etc. People use dustbins only scrupulously for depositing waste etc. We find there clean atmosphere everywhere.

Pride of Place for Indian Engineers

Not all people living in America are rich. There are unemployed people and also vagabonds living there. There are people who are without homes. Sometimes we see people holding a small placard stating, "Help as much as possible". In such a group we find some Americans as well as people who had come from Mexico and black people. Those who have completed technical studies in India get here an average of Rs.2 to Rs.4 lakhs per month. Therefore, Computer Engineers from India are able to buy costly houses and pay high rent for residences. They are also able to give good education to their children. But people from Mexico or China, or black people do not have much income and have jobs in construction work, pipe-laying, working in commercial centres etc. Generally Americans are a little sore that Indian Engineers have increased house rent and the price of houses.

"Click or Ticket" Traffic Regulation

Cement and tarred roads are maintained very well. The residential places adjoining Freeway or Highways are protected by walls so that general public and cattle do not face any danger from fast moving vehicles. Vehicles which over speed the limits are tracked by police patrol vans through radar and action taken against transgressors. As vehicles involved in accident or in a break-down condition are immediately removed so that traffic is not disrupted. All must wear seat-belt. We find the police caution, "Click or Ticket" in many places. Drivers of vehicles always slow down, allow pedestrians to cross the road and then alone proceed in their vehicles.

Special Concession for Disabled

We find women drivers almost in equal number as male drivers in passenger buses. We find in buses and trains passengers carrying bicycles which they would use to go to their work spot. There are facilities in the front side of the buses to carry these cycles. In buses only drivers would be there. Disabled people are carefully placed within the bus using a battery operated hydraulic steps. This responsibility is borne by the drivers which they do with a humanitarian concern. In public places where there are rest rooms and separate toilets for men and women, provision is made for disabled as well. Similarly in roads, for the benefit of disabled persons special provision is made; places are marked in blue colour to indicate they could park their vehicles there. Other vehicles are parked in places where it is painted green. If the place is painted red, it means no parking there. We also find trained dogs leading visually handicapped crossing the road. Such scenes touch our hearts.

Recreation Parks

A novel feature in recreation parks is the provision of coke ovens so that families can cook and eat their meals. When men and women or lovers engross themselves in each other's company, others do not take cognisance of it. No 'moral-policing' as we find in our place. A "Scenic Railway', big roller-coaster created in 1924 in Santa Cruz beach is still maintained and it inspires awe.

Quick action by the Police

When I was in Freemont city, one evening I was spending time with relations in Elizabeth Park. At that time we heard the sirens of police vehicles in nearby streets. After sometime we saw a helicopter hovering above and landing in the middle of the street. On enquiry we learnt that a three year old child had slipped from third floor of a building and the police vehicle and helicopter had come over there to assist the distressed parents who had sent a message requesting help. The life of the child was saved. We could see how police help came very swiftly.

Police Excess

At the same time, on May 7, ABC TV news showed that on May 3 in Philadelphia state on hearing the shocking news of a police sergeant shot dead by some assailant, four policemen in a patrol van beat up mercilessly three innocent young men who were travelling in a car. I also saw the public reaction in condemning the action of the police. Public opinion was invited to be expressed through an email survey regarding the incident asking people to grade it as good, fair or bad. Police actions are thus immediately assessed.

Infrastructure of Industrial Units

There is a place called Sunny Valley. A large number of computer companies function here. Provision is made by the companies to run special trains for their employees who can be shared by the general public as well. For example there is a firm called cisco which has its own train and stations. But in our country government itself has to find and allot land and then infrastructure like roads, transport facilities etc. as it did in Taramani Tidalit Park which was done out of public money.

Craze for Computers

It will be no exaggeration if we were to say that Americans have become addicted to computers. One fourth of the computers in the world, i.e., 185 million computers are used in the USA. From children's computer games to business firm, schools and ordinary household's payment of electricity, telephone charges, rent etc. are all done through computers. Internet is a hobby in USA. Only after USA come states like Japan, Germany, China and England. Online business operations in 2004 accounted for 43 billion dollars according to statistics: this gives us an idea about extensive use of computers in business.

Cine Fields, a Comparison

In America 847 persons out of 1,000 have own TV sets. Only in our country more than 1,000 films are made per year. Even American comes only second with 633 films per year: Japan produces 300 films per year and France 160. From this we learn that the craze for cinemas is more in our country than even in advanced countries like America, Japan and France. As a result the attention of our youngsters is focused more on films; it is no exaggeration to say that consequently our national development suffers. In America people like **Bill** Gates, proprietor of Microsoft are earning enormous wealth and great industrialist like Rockefeller create charitable trusts endowed with several billions of rupees to implement plans in health, education, social security, wiping out illiteracy etc. We do not see any big cine actor industrialist in our country spending so lavishly on charities. But those who call themselves superstars want their fans to sing their praises only: we also see people of Indian-descent industrialists, who are among the richest in England, buying costliest residences for their sons.

Realisation of Bharati's Dream of Women's Freedom

The dream of Revolutionary poet Bharati, and Social visionary Thanthai Periyar that Indian women should be free to manage their households has been realised by Tamil women in America. Husband and wife go to jobs. When the husband goes to job responsibilities like leaving children and bringing back children from schools, buying provisions for the family, using car to go to banks and other places, sometimes leaving the husband on his way to job by dropping him at railway station or bus stations, are all done by the wife. The first thing they do after coming to America is learn to drive car and obtain licence.

Educational institutions are closed for summer vacation in America from the middle of June to September. Women want their confinement time to coincide during this holiday. They want their children to be born in America to get the status of American citizenship. Because it is not so easy to get citizenship. People have to wait between 7 and 10 years after working in the States to get citizenship.

Cine Halls which are breath-taking in Splendour and Magnificence

In Union City there are 25 theatres known as "Century 25" along with shops in a complex. In one of them a new film, "Indiana Jones and Mystic Crystal Kingdom" was being shown. I went to see it. One has to book 'e' ticket. Elders are charged 10 dollars and children 7.5 dollars. There are no different tariffs in ticket depending on where one sits as in our theatres.

Steven Spielberg has produced this film. Harisson Port, a prominent actor is the hero. His income is the highest in the world among cine stars, 3.25 thousand crore dollars! The picture is about how American and Russian experts compete with each other to unravel the mysterious secrets in South America. In the end it is depicted that Americans win. It is no exaggeration to say that Hollywood films encourage American dominance over others.

I could see some cars carrying national flags. Also in some cars I saw slogans like "Support American troops in Iraq". May 26 is observed as the Memorial Day for the deceased soldiers and it is declared a holiday. In our country generally no permission is granted to put up national flags in houses or business firms or vehicles. It does not mean that we are less patriotic. However, if permission is given to adorn the house or other places with national flag, from the very childhood patriotic fervour will grow.

Importance of Agriculture

Great encouragement is given for agriculture in America. Special encouragement is given for non-use of pesticides in agricultural operations. Nearly 40 percent of the total world production of maize is grown in America. The vegetables grown are preserved in good condition and are sold in air-conditioned super-markets. They are also taxed much. But once in a month there is a system called "Farmers' market" where farmers directly sell their vegetables to customers in a common place having their own tents. No tax is levied on purchases there. But when we find that in Tamil Nadu we have permanent blocks for Farmers' market where the farmers directly sell their produce to public without middlemen eating away much of the profit, we have only to appreciate the same.

Who is going to win?

In America, there is a Presidential form of government. Here only those who belong either to Democratic Party or Republican Party could become the President. The President enjoys 'veto' powers over some legislation. By using he can prevent the passage of bills passed by the majority in the Senate or the House of Representatives. The people who had migrated from England had settled in the coastal areas initially and subsequently drove the Red Indians who were the original inhabitant into the interior forest. Thereafter many black people were brought from Africa as slaves and were used to construct roads, houses, factories etc. So far only the Whites have been the Presidents of America. Presidents who wanted to give equal rights to the blacks like Abraham Lincoln and John F. Kennedy were assassinated. Similarly Martin Luther King Jr. who struggled greatly for citizenship rights of the Blacks and was identified as one who could become the first black President was short dead in 1964. But basket ball players like Michael Jordan, Abdul Kareem Jabbar, Sprinter Karl Leis, Golf player Tiger Woods, baseball players Beily Bont and Gong Asran and Three times world Heavy weight champion Mohamed Ali who brought hall of fame to America through their skills are only blacks.

This year in November elections to the President's post are to take place. To get the Democratic Party's approval for standing as the Candidate there was stiff competition between Ms.Hillary Clinton wife of former President Bill Clinton and Barrack Obama, a black. Generally there would be public discussions between the candidates. Some times mudslinging also would be resorted to. There was a false propaganda that Obama's ancestors were Muslims of Kenya and when Obama once went to Kenya he wore the traditional Muslim dress and therefore he should not become American President. But Obama proved that in truth Obama's parents were Christians living in America and rebutted the false arguments.

A Christian Evangelist Pastor White was making big propaganda that as Obama was black, white racists were conspiring to prevent him from becoming the President. This did not add to the stature of Obama who had to intervene and announce that he did not support the propaganda of Mr. White. This led to increase of support for him among the whites. Subsequently he was able to gather enough majorities and won the nomination on behalf of the Democratic Party.

Each candidate gets as donations to election fund millions of dollars. On behalf of Republican Party, John McCain is contesting as the candidate. Generally no American President would participate in any fund-raising programme. When Mr. George Bush announced that he would participate in one programme, it surprised American people.

But the prospective candidate of Republican Party, Mr. McCain did not announce that Mr. Bush would participate in the fund-raising programme. He knows that the popularity of Mr. Bush has declined considerably. Not even one out of four Americans support his policies. Mr. McClellan, who was the spokesman of the President has recently written a book in which he has stated that Iraq War was a big political mistake. This needless war has cost several billion of dollars loss and has strained American economy. Already there are complaints that Bush administration did not do enough in New Orleans state which had to face the ravage inflicted by hurricane Katrina. Moreover there is a general feeling that not much is being done to relive unemployment problem. The dollar is also very weak. These factors lead to the speculation that the Republic party might face defeat in the elections.

To compensate for these negative factors, Mr. Bush very much wants to conclude an Indo-American treaty on nuclear co-operation which would pave the way for US domination on India, which is a fast-growing nation. He thinks that would help McCain win the elections. However the Indian left communists are against Indian Government coming to an agreement with

USA. They also withdrew their support to Congress Party led UPA Government which forced the latter to seek a 'confidence vote' in the parliament, which it was able to win.

Mr. Barrack Obama at last worn not only the Presidential race of American in Nov. 4, 2008 but also the hearts of the people world over by unassuming simplicity, dedicated social service, presentation of his future policies vividly through his powerful oratorical sill and also emphasising the human fraternity and brotherhood. He created a psyche called 'OBAMAMANIA' in the Universe.

72

Intelligent Gay Excels International Bikni Killer Charles Sobharaj

Many of us may have come across the traits of International 'Bikini Killer' Charles Sobraj. He is a French national holding many passports of various nationalities in fictitious names. His modus operandi was to visit various tourist centres, befriend the tourists, kill them, and then steal away the passport, drafts, cheques, hard currencies, credit cards and utilize them for his purpose and then abscond. He was elusive on Interpol net. Finally he was caught at Nepal over a killing of an American tourist in 1975, sentenced to undergo life imprisonment and languishing in prison at Kathmandu. Similarly one young Crime Serpent, Senthil, in Tamilnadu had surpassed Charles Sobraj in cheatings over the heavy political weights and hardened criminals. Senthil Kumar aged 30 was a son of a farmer from Myladudurai village which is 300 km away from Chennai. He is 5´5" with medium built having wheatish complexion. His head is oversized from his body. He has got peculiar hawkish look which can see in two directions at the same time. He studied MBA course at Annamalai University at Chidambaram which is 100 km away from his native. He was a hostelite. While staying in the hostel he had not only become homosexual but learnt the art of cheating his room-mate telling him that he would tell his Professor to get him passed in the internal assessment. In addition he deceived his Professor that he knew the Pro-Chancellor of the University, Mr. M.A.M. Ramasamy and his Personal Assistant Mr. Rajendran and he would ensure that he would get the Head of the Department for him very soon so as to get good marks in the internal mark for the project. After graduating MBA, he indulged in petty cheatings in his native village inviting the wrath of his Dad to drive him away.

After graduating M.B.A, he indulged in petty cheatings in his native village inviting the wrath of his Dad to drive him away. With few bucks on hand Senthil came to Chennai in search of a job and took shelter in Excellent guest house at Triplicane which is a central place where the favour seekers would stay because of its proximity from the location State Secretariat. Staying at Chennai had turned Senthil a Crime Maestro. He made friendship with the manager of the lodge and through him he came to acquaint with the names of DMK party men who made beeline of seeking favours. At that time DMK was the ruling party in Tamilnadu from 1996-2001 May. He told to them that he was very intimate to Mr. M.K. Stalin, son of

DMK President, who was Mayor of Chennai city then, and he would likely to get engaged with the daughter of the Mayor. That way he was eking out his livelihood with what ever money he could extract from them. In the Non-Assembly days it was a difficult period for Senthil to get something for the stomach. On such occasions he used to stroll around Marina beach to entice gay members and flirt with them behind Catamaran of fishermen and get paltry amounts for his survival.

Marina beach is a sprawling four km stretch situated on the shore of the Bay of Bengal on East Coast. It is considered as the longest beach in Asia. One of his strolling he befriended one Mohan Babu of Perambur, who was an Attendant to the Chairman of Chennai Mylapore Permanent Finance Fund. Senthil showed the taste of homosexuality to him. Senthil pretended that he hailed from a wealthy family, closely knit with Pro-Chancellor of Annamalai University and well connected with ruling higher ups. He further told that his relative was working with the Central Secretariat with Mr. L.K. Advani, then Union Home Minister. In order to prove his closeness with Mr. M.K. Stalin family Mohan Babu used to get calls as spoken by Mr. Udayanidhi, son of Mr. M.K. Stalin enquiring about Senthil. One day Mohan Babu took Senthil to his Mylapore Permanent Fund Office. While he was sitting there Senthil's hawkish eyes saw Chairman, Mr. M.K. Balan, the neatly dressed in spotless white clothes. Senthil ascertained from Mohan Babu about the background of Mr. M.K. Balan.

Mr. Balan was a Dada in Mylapore locality having my hirelings, whose help the land developers used to seek to get the encroachers evicted. He got elected as MLA through AIADMK ticket from Saidapet Assembly constituency during 1991-1996. After the party met the debacle in 1996 election and DMK party ascended to the power he joined DMK party and became the Chairman of Mylapore Permanent Finance Fund. Even though he was married having 3 sons and a daughter he was maintaining one Lawanya daughter of Lalitha who came to seek favours from him as his mistress like many other politicians. Eventhough Mr. Balan was the partner in the chain of liquor shops he was greatly in debts to financiers.

M.K.Balan

The diabolic and crafty Senthil planned to get money from Mr. Balan. He told Lalitha that he would get Rajya Sabha M.P. Seat to Mr. Balan by using his good connection with Mr. M.K. Stalin family if he spares Rs. 10 Crores. Believing Senthil's version, innocent Lalitha and Mohan Babu arranged a rendezvous of Mr. Balan with Senthil at Partha Sarathy Temple Mandapam.. Shrewed Balan on seeing Senthil rejected him as a petty cheat and admonished both Lalitha and Mohan Babu for having friendship with Senthil. Stung by snubbing of Balan, enraged Senthil unleased another story to Mohan Babu telling him that Balan owed Rs. 8 Crores to Industrialist and Pro-Chancellor Mr. M.A.M. Ramasamy and he was instructed by him to get the money by utilising the services of rowdy elements. Suddenly it came to the mind of Mohan Babu about the name of on K.K. Nagar DMK functionary Dhanasekaran, who also runs a security agency. Both Senthil and Mohan Babu met Dhanasekaran in his office and told him about the extracting money from Balan and for which he would be given the commission of Rs. 50 lakhs. On hearing the version of both and the person's stature the Toughie Dhanakeseran drove the both out of his office. Immediately he also contacted Balan and cautioned him. The over confident Balan once again rejected it as a biggest joke and not warranted any attention. He had also dismissed Mohan Babu from the Attendant post.

Jaya Kumar

Stung by his repeated failure, Senthil was waiting for a soft prey. He noticed one Jayakumar, one time DMK student wing functionary visiting Triplicane Excellent Lodge and talking with DMK functionaries. Jayakumar already knew Mohan Babu, since he was working with Balan.. Jayakumar was residing at Anna Nagar along with his wife, mother and brother. He used to move along with an important party functionary and Minister in Anna Nagar. Even though he was doing small contract works he spent lot of money to the party work and started suffering from financial difficulties. His house was mortgaged and the financiers had issued notices for the auction of the house also. He came to know through Mohan Babu the age old story that Senthil was related to M.K. Stalin and he would likely to get engaged with his daughter soon. It drew a lot of respect for Senthil from Jayakumar who started to bring many party functionaries like Hariharan of Chintadaripet, Christopher and Vivekanandan doing small business. Among them the intimacy Senthil with Hariharan became thicker because of his homosexual relations. Hariharan had an Anglo-Indian wife due to love marriage and twins with deaf and dump.

Since State Assembly elections are scheduled shortly Senthil wanted to exploit many people who started queuing at DMK party HQ Arivalayam. Senthil Kumar and started loitering the broad lawns of Arivalayam pretending to Jayakumar and Mohan Babu that he was very closure to the party high command. He found Dhanasekaran of K.K. Nagar visiting Arivalayam for a party ticket in Saidapet constituency. He sent Jayakumar and Mohan Babu to the office of Dhanasekaran with the promise of getting an M.L.A. ticket. The bluffing of Senthil did not impress the over cautious Dhanasekaran. He immediately verified from the office of Mayor M.K. Stalin and found out the false story. He and his men thrashed Jayakumar and Mohan Babu heavily. That unforgettable incident had broken the confidence of Jayakumar against Senthil. But he could not leave Senthil altogether because he had spent considerable money to him as he was in greatly in debts. He took Senthil to his joint family home. His aged mother and wife were telling the story of their house was going for auction shortly. Senthil had promised them not to worry and he would arrange money since he was the relative Pro- Chancellor, M.A.M. Ramasamy by imitating that he was contacting him by his cell phone. It is very pity to note that the easy minds are nowhere nearer to the crafty fox. The Mother and Wife of Jayakumar believing his version showered all comforts to Senthil to the extent that they gave the well furnished room for Senthil and they were sleeping on the floor. Since Senthil did not arrange money as promised Jayakumar became restless. He went to the office of M.K. Stalin and verified the closeness of Senthil . The office staff told him that they had not heard of such person. Jayakumar informed Mohan Babu about the duplicity of Senthil.

Sensing that he was in trouble Senthil shifted his stay to the house of Hariharan at Chintadaripet. During his stay at Hariharan's house Senthil did not allow him to sleep with his wife. Senthil told that Sankaracharya was telling that having homosex was not an offence. Jayakumar met Senthil at Hariharan's house and told him that he would prefer the complaint against him to the Commissioner of Police if he did not part with his money. He was also serious in writing the complaint. It was August 23rd, 2001. There was the change of political guard in the State and AIADMK came to power. Sensing that he was in real problem from Jayakumar, Senthil caught hold of one Sami, Dada of Pulianthope, area and an AIADMK sympathiser through Hariharan. Senthil told Sami that he was closer to AIADMK circle and he was given assignment to extract money from certain people. Believing the version of Senthil as true, Sami mobilized his hirelings and kept ready for the command of Senthil. Sami was promised the heavy amount of Rs.30 lakhs for the job. Hariharan got Rs.90000/ from Selvarangan with the promise of employment and money was given to Senthil for kidnapping of Jayakumar and Mohan Babu. Senthil phoned up to Jayakumar to meet him at the appointed place in Thiruvanmiyur, busy commercial centre at 4 pm to collect the money. Anxious of getting the money back Jayakumar and Mohan Babu went in a motor cycle to that place and waited till night but Senthil did not turn there. Then Jayakumar got the call from Senthil asking him to meet him at Vadapalani, a cine-studio area of Chennai.

At about 8 pm some persons who came in an ambassador car approached Jayakumar and Mohan Babu telling them that they would take to meet Senthil. Without understanding the serious implications Jayakumar got into the car telling Mohan Babu to follow it in motor cycle. After reaching Virugambakkam, a suburban of Chennai, the gangsters took both Jayakumar and Mohan Babu inside to an old secluded house where Senthil and Sami were there. Jayakumar and Mohan Babu were confined and torture became. To add the salt to the injury, Senthil found the hand written complaint of Jayakumar to the Commissioner of Police against Senthil in his possession. Enraged over that, Senthil commanded Sami and his men to increase the tortures.

It lasted four days. At the end of the fourth day Jayakumar and Mohan Babu were directed to write letters to their homes telling that they were absconding themselves voluntarily in order to evade the pestering of the creditors. Both letters were sent by a courier. Then the gang shifted both to a farm house at Vandavasi, which is 120 km away from Chennai and confined. Senthil told both that having known that he was very closure to the Industrialist and Pro-Chancellor, M.A.M. they have spoiled the prospect of marrying the daughter of Mayor, M.K. Stalin. Then Senthil brought 'walkman recorder' and told the both to say that they were demanding Senthil to get favours from M.K. Senthil. By that time Mohan Babu fell on the feet of Senthil and entreated him to forgive because he could not bear the brunt of torture. But the hefty Jayakumar withstood the torture and defiantly waiting for the time, which did not because of his ill luck.

The gang took both of them to Kodaikanal, a hill station which is 600 km away from Chennai in an ambassador car and a Tata Sumo vehicle and lodged in a lodging house on 12th Sept, 2001. Senthil did not want to forgive the defiant Jayakumar. Next day morning Jayakumar and Mohan Babu were taken out to a nearby public call office and directed them to contact their wives at Chennai telling them that they would return home soon. In the evening Senthil told Jayakumar that DMK President had come to Kodaikanal for rest and he would take him to meet him in person. Jayakumar, even though DMK Student one time leader never met its President. Flushed with the ray of good future Jayakumar got ready to meet him. Senthil brought a bouquet and took Jayakumar along with Sami and gang in Tata Sumo on the pretext of meeting DMK President on 14th September, 2001. Jayakumar was holding the bouquet through out the journey. The Tata Sumo drove out of the town and passing through the famous suicidal point, a steep hillock. On reaching a secluded spot they stopped the Sumo car and all got down. Jayakumar grew suspicious and questioned them.

Immediately Jayakumar was gagged and attacked with logs, dagger and knife killing him. Then they pushed the body into the deep valley and threw their weapons and returned to their lodge telling Mohan babu that Jayakumar had left to Chennai last evening. The next morning they checked out the lodge and drove to Chennai. The gang dropped Mohan Babu at Christopher house warning him for serious consequences if he revealed anything. Sami and the gang put Senthil at Cresent Lodge in busy market area NSC Bose Road at Chennai and returned to their homes telling Senthil to arrange the promised money of Rs. 30 lakhs owed by Senthil for the gruesome murder of Jayakumar.

The badly beaten Mohan Babu did not go to his immediately since he got the bruises all over the body. Till all of them got healed he stayed in the house of Christopher for two weeks. In the meantime Jayakumar's family members visited the house of Mohan Babu in Perambur making enquiries of both. Mohan Babu returned home badly shaken. The non-arrival of Jayakumar from Kodaikanal and the search by his family are news for him. Then he informed to the family of Jayakumar that he must be with Senthil.

Sensing serious problem Jayakumar's brother complained to Anna Nagar Police Station in October, 2001 stating that his brother was missing for one and half a month suspecting the foul play from Senthil. Initially a man missing case was registered and there was no breakthrough in the investigation.

Hard pressed for money to diminish the wrath of Dada Sami and his gang and also for his own survival Senthil was on the look out for a powerful thug to kidnap M.K. Balan, who had snubbed Senthil on several occasions. Senthil thought that Balan would be having lot of money because of his position in the Mylapore Permanent Finance Fund. Senthil came to know that there was one notable AIADMK party functionary, Poonga Nagar Manikam, having his office in the busy commercial locality, N.S.C. Bose Road in which Cresent lodge where Senthil was also staying was located. Manickam was once close aide of the Senior AIADMK Minister, Mr. S.D. Somasundaram. Once Mr. S.D. Somasundaram fell out from the Party High Command, he was dropped from the Ministership when AIADMK was in power between 1991-1996. Manickam was also sidelined by AIADK party leaders and cadres. He always wore white safari. He had a band of undesirables. He was longing for an honourable place in the party at North Chennai. During 2001 May Assembly election AIADMK came to power defeating DMK. Having known Manickam's background, Senthil invented an idea to realize his dream of getting money from Balan by utilizing the services of Manickam. There is a female aide Madame Sashikala shortly called as 'Sashi' to AIADMK party President, who used to stay at her residence called 'Poes Garden'. Senthil had convinced Hariharan to make his wife Romita to imitate like 'Madame Sashikala' so he can rope in Manickam to act according to his tunes.

Without knowing the serious consequences Romita obliged her husband and Senthil calling Manickam in his cell phone as 'Madame Sashikala' telling him that Senthil was the cousin of the Special Adviser to Shri L.K. Advani, then Union Home Minister and he and Hariharan been given specific instruction to be carried and they would brief him in details. Overjoyed with the call from the so called power centre of AIADMK, Manickam thought that it was a golden opportunity to realize his long cherished dream of making successful re-entry to AIADMK and decided that he would do whatever Senthil commanded. The meeting between Senthil and Manickam was arranged at famous Star Hotel 'Connemara'. Senthil explained to Manickam in crisp that M.K. Balan had ditched AIADMK party high command by joining DMK during 1996-2001, amassed lot of money and it was intended to get back from him. Manickam promised that he would prove his loyalty to the Party High Command and showered all comforts to Senthil by accommodating at 'Excellency Hotel' in South Usman Road of

T.Nagar in a commercial area, with a car and an aide Balamurugan for his beg and call. Hari had also stayed with Senthil.

True to his words Manickam quickly collected a group of hardened criminals like Somu, who has got 16 criminal cases including 2 murders, Irudhi, who was involved in the dare devil murder inside the Chennai court complex, Sampath with 3 cases of murder to his head, Ramesh facing a murder case trial, Guna from Madurai-Dindigul a hardened criminal with a murder case, Bomb Selvam and Shankar and few other small time rowdies. Manickam further mobilized the support of his friends Udaysakumar, Venugopal, Venugopal and Krishan Pandy of Tambaram area to find out a place to confine M.K. Balan in case of his kidnapping. Finally they selected the vermicelli factory of Krishnapandy at Tambaram. Udayakumar arranged a fleet of two Maruti vans, a Ford escort car and a motor bike.

In the third week of December, 2001 Senthil made Romita to call Manickam as Madame Sashi instructing him to carry on the job and get the money back from M.K. Balan. On 26th December, 2001 evening while M.K. Balan was going in his car to his farm house at Kelambakkam in Old Mahabalipuram Road, where the software companies are located, from his Mylapore Fund Office, his vehicle was followed by the gangsters in the Maruti Omni van. The driver of Balan informed him on seeing through the side mirror. But Balan dismissed it casually. In the busy evening traffic mix-up the gangsters lost sight of the car of Balan. Then the gang started the recce of his daily schedule. Then they found that he was the regular early morning walk goer at MRC Nagar, a posh locality in the seashore.

The deadline of his trap was laid on 30th December 2001. Bomb Selvam surveyed the stretch of MRC Nagar in his motor cycle in the early morning onwards. One group led by Somu was waiting at MRI Nagar in a Maruti van. Second group stationed in a Ford Escort car at a distance. As usual Balan started from his residence in Mylapore wearing Reebok glittering shoes at about 5 am on 30th morning which was a foggy winter day. One Nirmal, a morning walker notice Balan when he passed him by his quick stride. He was then noticed by on Sudhakar, a boxer trainee at a distance. He noticed a Maruti van with slide door open closely followed Balan. Two occupants of the van got down and pushed Balan inside and sped away in a fraction of the second. The hefty Balan was subdued by the gang in the van like lame duck. He did not know who were his kidnappers and the purpose of their action.

The gang informed Manickam immediately. Then the swift chain of action began of vacating the first floor of vermicelli factory, furnishing an iron cot, bed pan, table fan and few chairs. The windows were covered with curtains. The employees were given holidays on the eve of New Year celebrations. Balan blind folded was brought to the first floor of vermicelli factory and chained in the iron cot and guarded one by one. Senthil visited the factory with a cassette recorder and started demanding from Balan Rs.16 crores. Balan explained his inability saying that he was in debts to financiers. Then Senthil told Balan to list out his properties and started recording. While the recording was in the midway Manickam appeared on the scene and the cloth covered on the eyes of Balan was removed. Balan was stunned to see the crafty fox responsible of his kidnapping none other than Senthil, who had been snubbed by him earlier. Finding himself exposed Senthil slipped away from the scene with the cassette. Manickam was visibly upset since he was not able to extract anything from Balan. When Balan did not return after his morning walk Manimaran, Balan's son reported with Foreshore Police Station. Rumours went round in the city that Balan was confined in a hotel room in Neelankarai, a suburb of Chennai city on the east coast road with the help of the S.P. of St.Thomas Police district. Manimaran rushed there on 31st and found none. In fact police conducted surprise check of all lodges along the East Coast on the eve of New Year and rounded up the trouble shooters.

Senthil did not want to leave Balan. On 31st December morning Senthil induced Romita to speak to Manickam like Madam Sashi commanding him to eliminate Balan if he was not forthcoming to part with any money. It had once again boosted the low morale of Manicka. He called up Somu and commanded him to kill Balan. In the evening the cloth covering the eyes of Balan was removed and he was told that he would be dropped at his home. In order to get ready one member shaved the face and thick mustache of Balan. The gang thought if Balan was killed and transported in a van he would be identified through his mustache if it was subjected by checks by the police enroute.

Balan was gagged and strangulated to death. The iron cot in which Balan was confined bore the brunt of the struggle of Balan while he was strangulated and it got dents. Maruti van was brought to the factory with a coffin to transport the body of Balan to the cremation ground at Perambur. Manickam approached the Attendants of Perambur Cremation ground near his house telling that his relative of 61 year old died due to prolonged illness in the General Hospital and he had to be cremated in the night. After sensing that Chennai City would be plunged in New Year celebration and the most of the policemen would be posted for bandobust in the main entertaining centres, beach and main roads, Somu gang waited past midnight on 31st of December. Then the gang drove the Maruti van with the body of Balan from the outskirts of Tambaram to Perambur avoiding the main arterial roads. On reaching the crematorium the Maruti van was driven inside. The caretakers saw the middle aged body of Balan instead of an old man of 61 years as told by Manickam and they raised the objection. Somu did not expect it. He brought the van outside and telephoned to Manickam who rushed there and convinced the caretakers that he would hand over the death certificate in the morning and he greased their palm. While Manickam was inside the crematorium, Somu gang opened the liquor bottles and celebrated their New Year achievement. At that time two policemen in cycle passed that way. They questioned their presence there in that odd hour. Somu outwitted them by telling that they were finishing their New Year carnivals. If the policemen had looked into the van they would have seen the body of Balan and the sensational case would have been detected by arresting the some criminals on the spot. But the lack of the dedication and seriousness in the duty missed the golden opportunity. After policemen left the scene, unscathed criminals took the body inside and cremated.

Next morning Manickam contacted Kamaraj, an attendant of General Hopital for a death certificate. He had also helped Manickam in getting the death certificate from a Doctor in the name of Rajamani Chettiar aged 61without knowing criminal implications. Further Manickam directed Sami to hand over the death certificate to the Attendants and also collect the ashes from the graveyard so the remains of Balan burnt body were not left. Duty bound Sami reached the crematorium, handed over the death certificate, collected the ashes and immersed them in the sea at Thiruvetriyur. In order to screen the evidence Somu gang returned to the Vermicelli factory, cleaned up the premises and reassembled the things in the first floor. The dented metal cot in which Balan was tied strangulated was dumped in the store room. Bomb Selvam, one of the accused took the Reebok shoes worn by Balan lying in the corner since they looked attractive.

The city newspapers and electronic media splashed the news of the about the missing of Balan and rumours were agog. Chennai city police were chasing the wild goose without any useful clue. After the crime Senthil, Hari and Romita reached the residence of Romita. Since Hari and Romita did not go home for New Year celebrations, Hari was admonished by his mother-in-law and sent away for a bad company with Senthil. Then Hari and Senthil took shelter in the house of Romita's uncle. The guilty conscious Manickam started pestering Senthil to take him to 'Poes Garden' to meet Madame Sashe as promised without knowing that they were empty promises. Senthil did not respond positively. There were also mutual bickering between Hari and Senthil and exchange of harsh words. On getting more suspicion on the genuineness of Senthil, Manickam and his gang members absconded. Similarly Senthil and Hari had also absconded. The ruling AIADMK government was under pressure to trace Balan and another DMK man Jayakumar. Hence DGP of Tamil Nadu had decided to transfer the case of Balan to CBCID in which I was a DIG for three years.

At that time I was undergoing Gender Sensitization training on 10.1.2001 and 11.1.2001 at Trichy which is 300 km away from Chennai.

While we were taking lunch on 11.1.2001 during break Mr. Amit Varma, IGP, called me and directed me to return in the night itself after the session was over since DGP ordered the transfer of the case to CBCID. I got permission from the course Director Madame Thilakavathy IPS, ADGP, I returned to Chennai in the night itself. I was having experience of working as Assistant Commissioner of Police and then Dy. Commissioner of Police, Law and Order. On 12.1.2002 at 1030 hrs I attended the joint meeting with S.P. Sridhar, another DIG, Mr. Dogra, IGP Mr. Amit Varma and ADGP Mr. Ramani. It was decided to form a special team under SP Mr. Sridhar and the investigation to be handled personally by DSP Mr. Venkateswaran. The special team traced Mohan Babu and interrogated. He narrated the diabolic act of Senthil, kidnapping of him and Jayakumar and confining of them at Kodaikanal. Then the man missing case of Jayakumar at Anna Nagar Police Station was altered into Kidnapping and torture. The team traced one Vivekanandan who was cheated by Senthil in getting back wife's stolen jewels. Vivekanandan pledged some of the remaining jewels of his wife and gave the money to Senthi, who made him to call Mohan Babu imitating as Udayaninidhi son of Mayor Mr. M.K. Stalin. Selvarangan gave Rs. 90000/ to Senthil for favours which money he utilised to hire the vehicles, lodging and boarding at Chennai Virugambakkam, Vandavasi and Kodaikanal. Christopher narrated the return of Mohan Babu from Kodaikanal with bruises all over the body. DGP had also transferred the case of Jayakumar from Anna Nagar Police to CBCID. A separate team under DSP Selvi Radhika was formed and it was pursuing the clue given by Mohan Babu with the help of Anna Nagar Inspector Mr. Kader Mohideen.

The missing of Balan and reward for good information were published widely in the city by pasting posters. We got information that Balamurugan, the driver of Manickam would have associated in the kidnapping. He was traced and put into newly installed 'Lie dectector' at CBCID office. He spoke of the conspiracy woven by Senthil in which Manickam and his gang had fallen prey to kidnap Balan and commit homicide and screne the evidence. It was ascertained that Manickam after absconding was staying at Kalakasthi, a temple town, on the way to Tiruppathi in Andra Pradesh. A team led by DSP Mr. Padmanabhan and SI. Mr. Krishnan Kutty were sent to bring him. Mr. Pon. Manickavel, SP.Chengai East Dist. against whom Manimaran s/o Balan had leveled allegation in early days after Balan's disappearance helped greatly in tracing Senthil and Hari. Then Sami, Somu, Sampath, Iruthi, Guna and other members were traced one by one. The vehicles used for kidnap and transport of body were seized. The cassettes with the voice of Balan on the fateful day were seized which corroborated the voice of Balan in the Board meeting of Mylapore Mutual Finance Fund. A list containing 12 names of prospective persons including Balan and Industrialist M.A.M. Ramasamy was seized from Senthil.

The glittering Reebok shoes of Balan were recovered from 'Bomb Selvam'. The cot in which Balan was confined bore the finger prints of the assailants present there. The nylon ropes, chains and knife were also seized. Perambur crematorium death register in which Balan was named as 'Rajamani Chettiar' and death certificate issued by General Hospital that Rajamani died over the heart attack issued by Doctor were also seized. The police constables who had spotted Somu gang sitting inside the van outside Crematorium and boozing were traced and they identified the accused. 108 witnesses and 103 documents and 39 material objects were filed on behalf of prosecution while laying the charge sheet at Fast Track Court. But the adamant Manimaran s/o Balan filed various petitions before the trial court and High Court telling that his father was alive and the political hierarchy with the help of local and CBCID police had not conducted proper investigation and pleaded to transfer the case for CBI inquiry. All his petitions were dismissed.

In the meantime the CBCID team led by DSP Selvi Radhika swung into action. They pursued the information provided by Mohan Babu and Vivekanandan. The sting operation to find out the missing of Jayakumar had started. The travel agency and private owner who rented the cars and Tata Sumo jeep to the accused to transport Mohan Babu and Jayakumar were traced and the trip sheets were seized. The drivers of those vehicles corroborated the version of Mohan Babu. The houses in which both of them were confined and tortured both at Virugambakkam and Vandavasi were found out and owners traced. The audio cassettes of the voice of Jayakumar and the hand written complaint of Jayakumar to the Commissioner of Police against Senthil prior to his abduction was seized.

The hotel at Kodaikanal in which Jayakumar and Mohan Babu along with Sami, Senthil and other gang members stayed were traced. The lodge inmates register which bore the entry of Senthil's signature was also seized. The lodge attendants identified the assailants, Mohan Babu and Jayakumar as stayed in the hotel in September, 2001. The confession of Senthil and Sami showed that Jayakumar was murdered and the body was thrown in the deep valley from the steep hillock. The Spl.Team with the help of the locals was able to locate the decomposed body by trying hard after 4 days. The clothes worn by Jayakumar, belt on the pant and the kerchief were found there. Accused identified the body. Jayakumar brother Babu and his wife Hemalalitha identified the clothes. The post mortem was conducted on the spot. The examination revealed that Jayakumar's skull bore the deep cut injury and cheek bones broken due to the beating with wooden logs. The skull and other materials were preserved for superimposition and DNA test which proved positive of Jayakumar's death. The kidnapping case was altered into homicide. 119 witnesses were examined, 117 exhibits filed and 58 material objects produced on behalf of prosecution.

While the accused were facing trial in the fast track court, Senthil Kumar who was lodged in Chennai Central Prison harboured an idea to extract money to meet the expenses of engaging an advocate for himself to defend. He told two ambitious prison warders that the owner of Nallamani Lodge located near Chennai Commissioner of Police Office at Egmore, namely Nallamani, owed some money to him and he instructed them to meet him and get the money as demanded by him. He had promised them for doing such job they would get commission. Enthused with the idea getting some amount both warders met Nallamani and demanded money as told by Senthil. Perplexed Nallamani winked at Prison warders and told them to wait. Since Nallamani was very familiar with Egmore police station staff he phoned up to the Inspector of Police from the ante room. The Inspector rushed there and arrested both warders. That case was also transferred to CBCID for further investigation. The innocent warders were also lodged in the same prison where they worked because of bad company with Senthil.

The cases of Balan and Jayakumar were tried by an upright Judge of Fast Track Court Mr. Ashokan. I and S.P. Sridhar attended important hearings. On 19th April 2004 the Judgements were pronounced. For the murder of Jayakumar, three main accused, Senthil Kumar, Hari and Sami were awarded two life imprisonments each and fine amounting in lakhs. The other members of the gang were awarded life sentence each along with heavy fine. For the murder of M.K. Balan, Ex.M.L.A., out of 18 accused 16 accused were convicted for life imprisonment with heavy fine. Senthil and Hari were convicted for two life imprisonments. The two accused escaped from the severe punishment were Romit, the wife of Hari, who was the victim of the circumstance and on compassionate grounds of maintaining her twin deaf and dump children and another Ganesan.

The historical Judgements once again vindicated the professional efficiency of CBCID teams under the experienced supervisory officers like IGP Mr. Amit Varma, SP Mr. Sridhar and I.

Index

S